The Thinking Manager's Toolbox

The Thinking Manager's Toolbox

*Effective Processes for Problem Solving
and Decision Making*

William J. Altier

OXFORD
UNIVERSITY PRESS
1999

OXFORD
UNIVERSITY PRESS

Oxford   New York
Athens   Auckland   Bangkok   Bogotá   Buenos Aires
Calcutta   Cape Town   Chennai   Dar es Salaam   Delhi
Florence   Hong Kong   Istanbul   Karachi   Kuala Lumpur
Madrid   Melbourne   Mexico City   Mumbai   Nairobi
Paris   São Paulo   Singapore   Taipei   Tokyo   Toronto   Warsaw

and associated companies in
Berlin   Ibadan

Copyright ©1999 by William J. Altier

Published by Oxford University Press, Inc.
198 Madison Avenue, New York, New York 10016

Library of Congress Cataloging-in-Publication Data
Altier, William J.
The thinking manager's toolbox : effective processes
for problem solving and decision making / William J. Altier.
p.   cm.   Includes index.
ISBN 0-19-513196-7
1. Problem solving. 2. Decision making. 3. Management.
I. Title. II. Title: Effective processes for problem solving and decision making.
HD30.29.A48   1999   658.4'03—dc21   99-28357

1 3 5 7 9 8 6 4 2

Printed in the United States of America
on acid-free paper

Contents

Preface

The Thinking Manager's Toolbox tells *how* to do a faster, more effective job of solving problems, making decisions, and planning. It offers proven thinking processes that can be easily used on an individual basis by anyone who wants to improve his or her executive or managerial batting average. They can also be used on a group basis by a task force or a team that wants to improve its effectiveness.

Not a week goes by without a major business-media story about a company that has gotten into trouble or an executive who has "resigned for personal reasons"—usually a euphemism for having done a less than acceptable job of problem solving, decision making, and planning. The majority of management failures happen because those involved didn't employ effective thinking processes in tackling the problems and decisions that they faced.

The Thinking Manager's Toolbox offers executives and managers and any and all breeds of problem solvers, decision makers, and planners a complete set of fundamental thinking processes they can use to handle any situation. Because these processes are based on the fundamentals of applied logic, they can be used in *any* type of situation.

The thinking processes offered in *The Thinking Manager's Toolbox* are excellent time reducers. Over and over, they have helped companies reach concrete, optimum answers in a few days, often for issues they had wrestled with for weeks, months, even years.

Most managers will immediately see the applicability of at least one of these thinking processes to an issue that is stagnating on their desks. However, that's only the first inning of a game that should be a lifelong quest to be better problem solvers and decision makers. Until managers become so proficient at applying these thinking processes that their use is second nature, this book will be a valuable reference tool that should always be close at hand.

The Thinking Manager's Toolbox would not exist were it not for my good fortune to have been employed by Kepner-Tregoe, Inc. (K-T) for eleven years. Founded in 1958, K-T offered training programs in the fundamental thinking processes of Situation Appraisal, Problem Analysis, Decision Analysis, and Potential Problem Analysis. These programs taught thinking-process tools based on systems of fundamental applied logic. The thinking processes are as old as the philosophies of Plato and Aristotle. Chuck Kepner and Ben Tregoe reinvented them; they translated them into modern everyday language, took them out of the abstract, and molded them into practical tools for applied thinking.

In the 1970s, K-T clients were increasingly asking for direct consulting assistance. They had major problems that they hadn't been able to solve; they had major decisions to make in which opposing organizational camps had let their emotions override their process training. I conducted most of these consulting assignments and thoroughly enjoyed them. However, at the time K-T didn't encourage such work. Strategically, they saw their business as being in training and development, not in consulting. Excited about these consulting experiences, and disenchanted with the repetitiveness of conducting training programs, in 1976 I decided to set out on my own. I set up Princeton Associates, Inc., to pursue this unique type of management consulting for which I had come to see a tremendous need.

This work quickly led me into the "real world," the world that the textbook processes didn't always accommodate well—situations that could be better handled by modifying the ideas presented in the management tome of the time, Kepner and Tregoe's *The Rational Manager*. These situations led to the development of new techniques and new concepts.

The Thinking Manager's Toolbox is the summation of the improvements that have been made over the years to the basic processes of Situation Appraisal, Problem Analysis, Decision Analysis, and Potential Problem Analysis. In several instances, it offers a significant advance in decision-making techniques and the analysis of business problems and opportunities. *The Thinking Manager's Toolbox* will help you to apply these improved processes to the real situations organizations face today.

Some Food for Thought

Chess is a game that is won by better thinking; so too is business. One doesn't become an expert chess player by reading books about the game; expert status is the result of repeated drill and practice, of continually playing the game and learning from one's mistakes. One doesn't become an expert business problem solver or decision maker by reading books on the subject; expert status is the result of repeated drill and practice, of continually solving problems and making decisions and learning from one's mistakes.

In an article titled "You Cannot Lead What You Do Not Understand — You Do Not Understand What You Haven't Done," Myron Tribus observed that:

> The great quality teacher, Shoji Shiba, often tells people that the biggest barrier to changing understanding is the following word: IAKI, which is not a Japanese word at all. It is an acronym for I ALREADY KNOW IT. . . . Professor Shiba then goes on to say: "Yes, you may *know* it, but you don't know how to *do* it!" There is an enormous difference between *knowledge* and *know-how*. . . . Too many executives believe that if they listen to a lecture or read a book they will know how to do something. . . . Nobody ever became a great lover by just reading a book or watching a video. You have to get in and do it. There are some things you can only learn through experience. (Myron Tribus, "You Cannot Lead What You Do Not Understand— You Do Not Understand What You Haven't Done," *Journal of Innovative Management*, Fall 1996.)

This book is written for people who want to become expert problem solvers and decision makers. Whether you call yourself an engineer, an executive, a homemaker, a leader, a manager, a problem solver, a secretary, a technician, a thinker, a troubleshooter, or whatever, if you don't bat 1.000 in your problem solving and decision making (do you know anyone who does?), this book can help you raise your batting average—significantly—*if* you are sufficiently disciplined to commit yourself to the effort required to do so.

Do *not* expect to master the concepts and techniques discussed in this book just by reading about them; mastery will come only as a result of actually applying them. I recommend that you read the text thoroughly and then use it as a reference tool each time you are confronted with a significant problem. If you take these processes to heart, and really learn how to use them, years from now you'll still be discovering exciting new ways to adapt and apply them. Following structured thinking processes shouldn't be a chore but a voyage of discovery and creative learning on the path toward greater organizational success and fewer crises.

Enjoy!

March 1999   W. J. A.
Buckingham, Pennsylvania

Acknowledgments

Interspersed between time spent on airplanes, it took a couple of years to create the manuscript for this book and transform it into a finished document. Along the way, many friends and professional associates reviewed drafts and offered insights on how to improve it. Many thanks are due to Russ Ackoff, Chris Argyris, Frank Bjornsgaard, Bud Erickson, Peter Hanson, Chuck Kepner, Elspeth MacHattie, Chuck Mitchell, and Gene Rickle for their time and efforts. I am deeply indebted to them, to Diane Ash who keyboarded hundreds of pages of my handwritten raw material, and to Herb Addison, Executive Editor at Oxford University Press, who persistently coached me through the final polishing. I am especially grateful to the many clients who enabled me to enhance these thinking processes by virtue of asking for help in resolving situations that weren't readily dealt with using the tools of the time, thus providing me with opportunities to make new discoveries.

The Thinking Manager's Toolbox

Part I

SETTING THE SCENE

Would you like to be able to:

- Help your people solve a problem in a few days that they've been unable to crack in three months—and one that has cost your company its lead market-share position?
- Come to consensus in a day on a critical decision that you—the CEO—and your Executive Committee have been wrestling with for over a year?
- Help an internal task force develop an answer to a $100-million problem that, after two years of effort, they said couldn't be answered?
- Have your next new product launch, or new plant start-up, be significantly more trouble-free and successful than any of your previous experiences?
- Determine how to restructure your organization so that your best people stop jumping ship?

The thinking processes that have been used to accomplish results such as these are revealed in the following pages. This first section makes a case for the value, importance, and comprehensiveness of the thinking tools that are discussed in practical detail in Parts II and III: Decision Analysis, Implementation Planning, Potential Problem/Opportunity Analysis, and Problem Analysis.

Why eat up time setting the scene? Many books have been written about a plethora of problem-solving and decision-making techniques, and the fact that people continue to write these books—some of them best-sellers—suggests that they have not accomplished their mission or made converts of their readers. Although they may offer excellent techniques, they may not have convinced their readers of the value of the techniques they proffer.

Don't waste your time reading Parts II and III unless you *believe* they can open new horizons for you. And yes, waste is the operative term. Unless you believe, you will not be committed to the effort required to internalize these concepts. Unless you commit yourself to investing the time and effort to internalize them, you will be wasting your time. This introductory section aims to make you a believer.

Chapter 1 shows you why organizations' struggles to succeed are *thinking battles*.

Chapter 2 demonstrates why change is the name of the game in modern management.

Chapter 3 illustrates how thinking-process expertise leads to problem-solving success.

1

Thinking Battles—Winning and Losing

Some Battles Won

This client enjoyed worldwide dominance in its product niche. A major competitor had been acquired by a company with extremely deep pockets. The client felt that the acquiring company intended to supply its competitor with funds to mount attacks on their lucrative market positions and wanted help in developing a plan to counteract this probable competitive move.

The project involved working with eight of the client's people for two days. First, they assumed the role of the competitor and, using Potential Problem Analysis, determined the competitor's most likely offensives and created scenarios of its probable actions. We then moved into a Decision Analysis mode and developed ways of preventing the competitor's presumed plans from ever getting off the ground.

The actions subsequently undertaken by the client as a result of this analysis were a resounding success. The competitor's attempts to cut into their market positions were completely blocked; about two years later the merger was dissolved.

Changing conditions in another client's major market dramatically reduced the demand for its specialized products. There was unanimous agreement that it had to condense the scope of its product line; however, there was a broad divergence of opinion as to how this should be done. The company appointed an internal task force to resolve the issue and expected that it would take them a year to come to a conclusion. The task force's initial meeting had been a disaster; the client asked for help.

Starting with a clean sheet of paper—and working with most of the client's original task force—in a two-day Decision Analysis a new product scope was developed that the group was tremendously excited about. However, they were afraid it was so radical that no one on the team wanted to be the messenger who delivered the message to their vice president. He was therefore asked to join the meeting; after a brief explanation of the analysis and its outcome, he enthusiastically endorsed it. His comment: "I doubt we could have reached the recommendation on our own—certainly not in two days."

Two critical concerns, each resolved in two days. Why do accomplishments like this have to be the exception rather than the rule? This chapter examines the paradox that all organizations want good decisions, yet most fail to apply the appropriate thinking processes to the issues on their plates.

Why Organizations Fail

The critical importance of effective thinking was expressed in Ben Heirs's *The Professional Decision Thinker*:

> We should expect those who direct our corporations and public institutions to be—in addition to possessing their other important skills and qualities—*professional thinkers*. For the battles we have been losing since 1960 have been, above all, *thinking* battles.[1]

I'm in complete agreement with Heirs's first sentence. However, I disagree with his chronology. Failure to apply effective thinking is not limited to the past few decades. The battles that business organizations have been losing since time immemorial have been thinking battles.

A corporate body, unlike its human counterpart, has the ability to replace failing organs at will in perpetuity. Corporate bodies don't wane or die because they lose a battle with cancer or experience kidney failure or whatever. Corporate bodies fade because they lose thinking battles and make poor decisions.

You've Been There

Most readers have probably participated in meetings of, say, six or eight people that were called to "solve a problem, make a decision." And you have probably been involved in situations in which every one of these six or eight attendees walked into the meeting with his or her mind already made up as to what should be done and each of the six or eight ideas was totally different. Finally, you have probably been involved in situations in which the idea ultimately "accepted"—if you could call it that—was one that came from the person with the loudest voice or the highest on the pecking order. This is an example of a thinking battle being lost.

Why do things like this occur? They happen because no systematic thinking process was employed to resolve the issue, because no one bothered to open his or her mental toolbox and pull out the appropriate thinking tool.

The Challenge of Objectivity

Every one of the people in these meetings was paid to think in terms of "What's best for the organization?" And yet each person's de facto perspective often is "What's best for my department, or for me, or for my ego?" When such a climate prevails, objectivity wanes and the organization loses.

One of the recent vogue terms in management is "core competencies." Hamel and Prahalad define this aspect of effective management as:

> A bundle of skills . . . that enables a company to provide a particular benefit to customers. . . . Core competencies are the soul of the company and as such they must be an integral part of the process of general management.[2]

But what about the core competencies of executives and managers, those who lead companies? Shouldn't we also say that:

> A core competence is a bundle of skills that enables an *executive* or *manager* to provide a particular benefit to *the company*. Core competencies are the soul of the *executive* or *manager* and as such must be an integral part of the process of general management.

If it is true that executives and managers need specific core competencies, then the most universally needed and critical competence has to be that of *thinking*, of having effective processes for analyzing the problems and decisions whose outcomes will ultimately influence the success, or failure, of the organization.

This book focuses completely and solely on this core competence.

The Intelligence Trap

Having the skill to use thinking processes is not the same as simply being "intelligent." Most executives and managers are intelligent, yet they fall into what Edward de Bono calls the "intelligence trap":

A highly intelligent person will take a point of view and then use intelligence to defend it. . . . Many excellent minds are trapped in poor ideas because they can defend them well. . . . People who are very intelligent want to get the highest, quickest payoff from their intelligence. This is often found by attacking someone else.

Traditional thinking is based on the adversarial system—one party seeking to prove the other party wrong.

A bad thinker who has a lot of experience becomes an excellent bad thinker.[3]

The intelligence trap tends to twist managers' thinking away from the real problems the organization faces; it leads to people losing their objectivity. Executives and managers also often lose their objectivity because of their closeness to a situation. Since they likely will be impacted by the outcome of the decision, they lack what psychologists refer to as "stranger value." Peter Drucker summed it up:

The executive in an organization . . . is like the physician who treats his own family—he diagnoses with the heart and always takes his own pulse rather than that of the patient.[4]

The length of time you take to hone and perfect your thinking skills is only one factor; it's your ability to *objectively* apply these skills that ultimately determines how effective you will be.

Managing = Manufacturing

The act of managing is in many ways analogous to the act of manufacturing. Just as manufacturing operations turn out products, so do managers; their products are called actions. For example, an automobile manufacturer starts out with various raw materials such as stampings, moldings, wire, and paint. These raw materials are then subjected to various processes such as welding, machining, assembly, and finishing. The result, as shown in Table 1.1, is a car.

Management also has its basic raw material: it's called information. A manager takes this basic raw material of his or her job and subjects it to various processes such as analysis and synthesis. The resultant outcome, as shown in Table 1.2, is one or more actions.

If we go back to the automobile portion of this metaphor, we see that the quality and quantity of the cars a manufacturer ships to its customers are a

Table 1.1. Result Model

Raw Materials	Processes	Result
Stampings	Welding	Car
Moldings	Machining	
Wire	Assembly	
Paint	Finishing	

Table 1.2. Result Model

Raw Materials	Processes	Result
Information	Analysis	Action(s)
	Synthesis	

function of the quality of the raw materials and the quality of the processes it uses (Figure 1.1.).

The same is true in managing. The quality and quantity of the actions that a manager outputs are a function of the quality of his or her raw material and the quality of his or her processes, as shown in Figure 1.2.

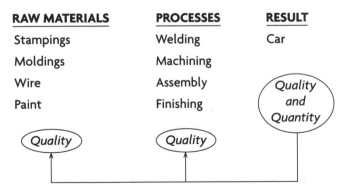

Figure 1.1   Result Model

What Every Process Requires

This book describes several different thinking processes. However, they all share a set of basic characteristics that are vital to their effectiveness:

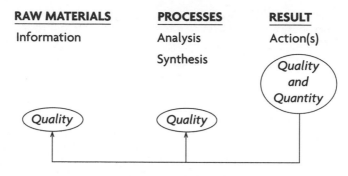

Figure 1.2   Result Model

A *process* enables people to take mental steps together.

A *process* is a necessary sequence of steps by which information and judgments are organized so that a conclusion can be reached.[5]

To be effective, a *process* must be:

- Rational
- Selective
- Universal.[6]

To be *rational*, it must follow a logical, step-by-step sequence.[7]

To be *selective*, it must include questions that uncover the relevant information necessary to complete each step in the process and which put aside the irrelevant.[8]

To be *universal*, it must function independently of the particular content to which it is applied. As the organizing principle of information and thinking, it remains constant.[9]

Thinking processes are applied to *problems*, which *Webster's* defines as "questions proposed for solution, decision, or determination."[10] Thinking processes can be divided into the two categories of analytic thinking and systems thinking.

The thinking processes illustrated in this book are universal—they are fundamental to consistently good problem solving. However, they are *not* a panacea; they are *not* the complete and total answer to *all* the world's problems; they do have their limitations because they are *analytic*. On the issue of crime, for example, the Problem Analysis process may be useful in determining why a particular person committed an initial criminal act or started using illegal drugs. However, it is useless in attempting to come to grips with the macro problems of "crime in America" or "illegal drugs in America." Problems such as these are *systemic* problems; they require the use of the tools of systems thinking, of synthesis, if they are ever going to be effectively dealt with. In systems-thinking terms, they are appropriately referred to as "messes."

Systems thinking solves problems through expansion; it moves to determine the components that interact with each other and how they affect the bigger picture. Analytic thinking solves problems through reduction; it moves to dissect problems into their discrete components.

Neither the governments of the United States nor all the governments in the world have sufficient resources to diminish crime and illegal drug use by applying analytical thinking tools to each and every perpetrator. If they did, then, by definition, these problems would not exist. The tools of systems thinking are the only hope for dealing with such messes.

The Excellent Thinker

The discussion so far suggests that excellent thinkers have a number of specific attributes. An excellent thinker is a person who can receive information, process it without too much delay, and draw logical conclusions from it *if* there are logical conclusions to be drawn. If logical conclusions are *not* called for, an excellent thinker knows why; he or she recognizes what the flaws are.

A process, by definition, involves a series of steps. Excellent thinkers know that these are not just randomly assembled lists of steps to follow; there are specific linkages between the sequential steps. They never forget that each step builds on, and evolves from, the information developed in the preceding steps.

The Decision Analysis process described in Chapter 5 has five steps:

1. Define the Decision Statement
2. Establish Objectives
3. Value Objectives
4. Generate Alternatives
5. Compare and Choose

The specifics of the objectives established in the second step should be controlled and constrained by the scope defined by the Decision Statement. The valuation of the objectives that is accomplished in step three should define the relative importance of each objective created in the second step. The scope of the alternatives created in the fourth step should be constrained by the Decision Statement. The fifth step, Compare and Choose, takes the alternatives generated in step four and evaluates them against the objectives valued in the third step.

Effective thinkers know that pursuing these steps out of sequence can have damaging consequences. Devoting time to thinking about alternatives before the objectives have been given thorough attention can lead to a set of objectives that—consciously or subconsciously—is a stacked deck; based on personal bias or knowledge, the objectives may favor a particular alternative to the detriment of achieving what is truly in the decision maker's best interests.

Every step in every process requires information. Seldom does a problem solver possess all the information that an analysis requires thus he or she often has to seek information from other people. This is done by asking questions. Excellent thinkers know that there is room for only one type of questioning in any and every process: tight, specific, directed, *open-end* questions. These are questions that can't be answered with a "yes" or "no"; they seek information, not what could be a judgment. Closed-end questions are ones to which people can respond yes or no; such questions often elicit an opinion, not information.

Excellent thinkers understand that even though they may not have all the information at hand that an analysis might require, the best thing is to get started. They go as far as they can and every time they come up against a process question that can't be answered, they put a big red question mark beside it. When they can't go any further because of information voids, they call time-out. They give specific information-gathering assignments to the team members, determine how long it will take to get the missing pieces, and then decide when they'll reconvene to crank in the missing information and complete the analysis.

An excellent thinker is a person who can approach an analysis with an open mind; one who can digest the information presented, separate the relevant from the irrelevant, and come to logical conclusions *regardless* of any prior knowledge about a situation or any perceptions, pet ideas, or biases. No one is immune to the disease of biases or preconception, but excellent thinkers have control over it; it doesn't control them.

The late Dr. Norman Vincent Peale extolled "the power of positive thinking," and such thinking clearly has its place in how people manage their lives. However, it's been my experience that excellent thinkers have an exceptional appreciation for the power of negative thinking too; they have a keen ability to uncover all sides, including the dark side, of the information they process.

Poor thinkers want to talk, to defend; good thinkers want to listen, to learn. Poor thinkers will jump to conclusions based on initial or superficial information, based on just enough information to support their biases. Good thinkers will arrive at conclusions only when they have adequate information to support them.

In time gone by, organizations revered people who always "knew the answer" and always had the appropriate information on the tips of their tongues. In other words, they revered knowledge. They proved it by paying the highest salaries to their college-graduate hires who had the highest grades—which often were the product of their having accumulated more knowledge than their fellow students, as opposed to their being better thinkers. However, times have changed. It is estimated that much of the knowledge possessed by engineers the day they graduate from college is obsolete within five years. Thus their long-term value to their employers lies not in their ability to regurgitate old knowledge, but in their capacity to think and acquire new knowledge.

2

Change: The Name of the Game

If you could build a new plant for the manufacture of cars, and

- if the vendors would always deliver the proper quantity and quality of their materials or components on time every time, and
- if the workers would never get sick or go on strike, if the machines would never break down or need adjustment, if there would never be any design changes, and
- if the customers would always want the same types and colors and quantities of cars every time, then
- you wouldn't need any managers in that plant.

By definition, you could open the door, turn on the lights, and walk away and the plant would do its thing perfectly. But that isn't the real world; in the real world we are continually confronted with that thing called *change*. And we've invented a special breed to deal with this thing called change; we call him or her a manager and expect this manager to use information effectively in the conduct of his or her job. But there's an important caveat about this raw material called information.

Managers aren't, or shouldn't be, concerned with all the information that floats around their job environs; they should only be concerned with information about change. This chapter describes the types of change that are important to organizations and matches these changes to specific thinking tools.

Two kinds of change are, or should be, of concern to management: past change and future change. Your immediate reaction may be "Hey, you forgot about the present." But there isn't any such thing as the present; the present is a fleeting knife edge, a microsecond in time. You picked up this book and started to read it in the past; that's an established fact. Your expectation is that you'll finish reading it in the future; that's an inference. It's not impossible that, before you complete this book, a devastating catastrophe—perhaps an earthquake—may send you on to your reward.

Yes, there's also a multitude of other prefixes to apply to the word "change," such as climate change, culture change, environmental change, technological change, and so on ad infinitum. But aren't these all components of past or future change?

Let's turn this concept into a model (Figure 2.1).

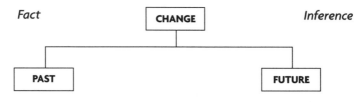

Figure 2.1   Change Model No. 1

Each of these two types of change can be dissected into two further types: planned and unplanned (Figure 2.2).

Let's take a deeper look at each of these four types of change and their implications for management.

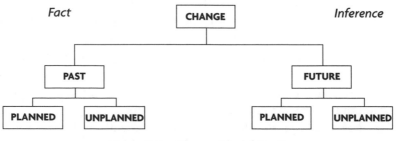

Figure 2.2   Change Model No. 2

Planned Past Change

"The merger with ABC Company completely met our objectives."

"The start-up of our new plant went according to plan."

This type of change is not of concern to management as far as any need to analyze it. It depicts a situation in which something that was expected or planned has happened; everything was on target. (Of course it's always possible that, in light of new information, an intended and accomplished Planned Past Change was wrong. If that's the case, then management must move to undo or change it via Planned Future Change.)

Unplanned Past Change

"The reject rate on product 102 doubled yesterday."

"Our sales in the Western Region rose by 50% last month."

This type of change should be of significant concern to management. It involves situations in which something didn't happen as intended. As a result, the organization faces a problem. Whether the actual change was undesirable or desirable, management's concern should be to find out why it occurred. Management must find the cause so that an undesirable change can be corrected or a desirable change perpetuated. To gather information about Unplanned Past Change, managers must use a specific thinking process called *Problem Analysis*. This is a process specifically structured to deal with factual information.

Planned Future Change

"We have to select a person to manage our new plant."

"We need to decide how we're going to finance the expansion."

This type of change should be of significant concern to management because the organization should be determined to make the best Planned Future Change from among the range of options available to it. Planned Future Change is nothing other than making, and implementing, a decision. There is a thinking process specifically structured to deal with the inferential information that surrounds the decision situation; it's called *Decision Analysis*.

Unplanned Future Change

"Competitor XYZ is going to merge with ABC Company."

"We should be able to launch our new product in six months."

Situations such as these should be of significant concern to management because they can bring trouble along with them. It's incumbent on management to do its best to anticipate such trouble and try to prevent it or, in the worst case, be prepared to react to it the instant that it happens. There's a specific thinking process structured to deal with such kinds of situations called *Potential Problem Analysis*.

On the flip side of the coin, Unplanned Future Change can also be a source of opportunity. It's also incumbent on management to do its best to anticipate such opportunity and promote its occurrence or, at the minimum, be prepared to react to it when it happens. There's a specific thinking process structured to deal with such kinds of situations called *Potential Opportunity Analysis*.

Back to the Change Model

Aligning these tools, these thinking processes, with the change model produces a model for selecting the appropriate process for each type of change. Thus the model itself becomes a tool, as shown in Figure 2.3.

Each of the three thinking processes introduced here is a tool, a tool with specific uses. A hammer works great with a nail, but it doesn't do much for a screw or a bolt; a wrench works great with a bolt, but it doesn't do much for a nail or a screw. Likewise, each of these thinking processes will produce

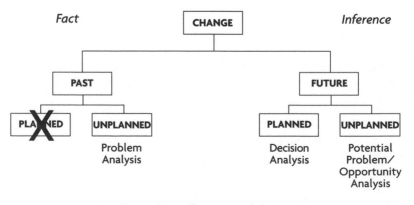

Figure 2.3   Change Model No. 3

the results managers need *only* when it is used for the particular type of change for which it's designed.

The second section of this book develops each of the thinking processes and shows you how each one works. But first it's important to continue to explore how fundamental, universal, and comprehensive these thinking processes are.

3

Process Expertise—A Critical Managing Skill

Effective managers design workable actions or policies for specific change situations by applying the relevant thinking process or processes to the situations. Although this is important, there's still more of a case to be made for applying thinking *processes* to managerial decisions.

Suppose you were faced with a life-threatening condition that required you to undergo major heart surgery. Whom would you select to perform this procedure? You've known your family physician for a couple of decades and hold her in the highest regard. After all, she was first in her class at medical school, interned at a prestigious, leading-edge hospital, and seldom does a year go by without her receiving some type of national accolade. But then, she's never performed the operation you need. The alternative is a specialist whom you've never heard of. By the way, he was in the same medical school class as your family physician and graduated in the bottom quartile. In the last ten years, he's performed the operation you need several times a week, with excellent results.

Which physician would you select to put you under the knife? Aside from the fact that your family physician would probably refuse to perform the procedure, most people would select the specialist they've never heard of. Why? Because this person has extensive knowledge of, and experience in, the *processes* that are required to successfully perform the operation. Not only is this person skilled in the required processes, most likely he is also skilled in a spectrum of ancillary processes that could be called for in case an unexpected problem developed during the course of the main surgical procedure.

An airline pilot who's been on the job for ten years has probably made thousands of takeoffs. He has gone through the same takeoff process more times than he can remember. And yet, despite his tremendous inventory of experience, he is still required, before every takeoff, to go step by step through a written checklist process to ensure that not a single vital element has been overlooked. Why? Because the experts in aviation know the importance of not skipping a single step in the *process*.

Many executives are avid golfers, but few if any are as good as Arnold Palmer or Jack Nicklaus were in their prime. Why? In most cases, it's simply because they don't have as much experience in such fundamental processes of golf as driving, chipping, and putting; they haven't been able to hone these skills to the point where their performance of the *processes* is world class.

Acquiring Process Proficiency

My *Webster's* defines managing as: "to control and direct . . . to conduct, carry on, guide, administer."[1] This sounds reasonable, but it doesn't say anything about decision making. Yet most who see themselves as managers would say, "Of course decision making is one of the most significant elements of managing."

The bottom line is that controlling and directing are accomplished by deciding things, by making choices. Most executives make more decisions in a day than they realize. Many of these, such as "Where should I take our visiting customer for lunch?," are routine and don't harbor serious risks. (But if your customer belongs to a religious sect with unique dietary beliefs, there could be significant risk lying in wait in this decision.) Others, however, such as "Which of these new product ideas should we go with?," have the potential to be "bet-the-company" choices.

The bet-the-company decisions are analogous to choosing the surgeon for the heart operation, a "bet-the-body" decision. In both cases, it would seem reasonable that such decisions should bring to bear the best skills and experience in decision making that are available. This ought to mean entrusting the decision to those who have mastered the *process* of decision making. And how does one master a process? By doing it on a continuing basis, just as the heart specialist, the airline pilot, and the professional golfer do.

Seasoned pilots use a checklist for every bet-the-airplane takeoff to confirm the process in which the pilots are already well experienced and skilled. The crash on takeoff of Northwest Airlines flight 255 at the Detroit airport on 16 August 1987 is a harsh reminder of what can happen when experienced pros fail to follow every step of a process. The National Transportation Safety Board attributed the cause of this crash to the pilot's failure to extend the plane's flaps and slats, which in turn was attributed to failure to follow every step of the pre-flight checklist. This was validated by the cockpit voice recorder, which revealed that the pilot, due to distractions, had skipped that step on the plane's takeoff checklist.

Many executives don't use a checklist for their bet-the-company decisions because they don't have one. In fact, few executives have extensive training and ongoing practice in the *process* of decision making. No doubt many were exposed to Linear Programming or Decision Trees or Force Field Analysis or a variety of other thinking processes during an MBA program. Perhaps some went through a Kepner-Tregoe program or similar training during their trip up the ladder. However, few continuously apply this learning to the critical decisions they resolve as a routine part of their job. Therefore, they don't develop proficiency in the process.

If you want to verify how easy it is to forget all the steps in a process you don't frequently use, get ten people who say they've changed a flat tire on a car to write down every step involved in the process. If you get one person who describes *every* step, in the proper sequence, you'll be lucky. Now you know why airplane pilots never stop using their checklists.

Judging Your Own Proficiency and Objectivity

Good decision making requires objectivity, not just in carrying out the thinking process but also in determining whether you are the right person to carry out that process. Process expertise is not a panacea. Decision makers can be confronted with situations in which it would be easy to let their emotions override their objectivity, thus rendering impotent any process expertise they may possess. When emotions and personal perspectives enter, objectivity can fade—and when it fades, disaster can loom. As the old adage goes: "A man who is his own lawyer has a fool for a client." When a person lacks distance from a concern, when he or she lacks stranger value, objectivity can become elusive and difficult to approach.

Most executives are like the family physician. They have become very good at being all things to all people; that's what's expected of them. However, while most family physicians wouldn't think of engaging in bet-the-body heart surgery, many executives will jump into bet-the-company decisions without batting an eyelash. Family physicians are trained to recognize the point beyond which their process expertise fades; they are also trained to recognize the role and value of those with specialized process expertise. They refer a patient to a specialist when they consider that action to be in the patient's best interests; they see this as doing what they're paid to do. Many executives feel an analogous action is *contrary* to what they're paid to do. They feel they get big bucks to make the big decisions all by themselves, and believe they are the only ones smart enough to do it right. Many see the use of specialists as an abdication of their responsibilities.

Using Specialists

It's a fact of life that—to paraphrase Professor Shiba quoted earlier—while executives may recognize the value of thinking-process expertise, being skilled in the application of such processes may not be their forte. Hence the value of employing the skills of process specialists in resolving critical issues.

The role of the specialist is *not* to solve the problem or make the decision; his or her role is to guide those who possess the relevant knowledge through the appropriate thinking process to help them come to an optimal conclusion. The specialist is an ally of the executives involved, not an adversary; together they form a winning team. They are two components of a winning equation. The thinking-process specialist helps those who are experts in the situation to maximize the effective utilization of their content expertise.

If you really apply yourself to learning the concepts offered in this book, if they become second nature to the point where their use is automatic, if you understand them inside out and upside down, if their use becomes a controlling element in the way you think, you could become a thinking-process specialist.

Trusting Intuition

Intuition is a warm, fuzzy term that many decision makers like to cuddle up to. It offers an easy—but not easily explainable—reason why a particular conclusion was reached. But just what is intuition? The dictionary defines it as: "Knowledge discerned directly by the mind without reasoning or analysis; a truth or revelation arrived at by insight; the power or capacity to perceive truth without apparent reasoning or concentration."[2]

Much day-in and day-out decision making is said to be intuitive, based on gut feel, experience, or whatever. Many decision makers defend a lack of process proficiency by extrapolating from the routine to the critical and saying that they make all their decisions intuitively. Two responses to this are in order.

First, the most important question to ask in a decision gone wrong is "What can we learn from it to prevent a recurrence?" A decision reached through the application of a specific process is a decision that followed a road map. If the organization arrives at what ultimately proves to be the wrong destination, it's easy to go back and examine the path that was followed to see where the wrong turn was made and learn from it. A decision reached intuitively has no visible record available for such reexamination or learning.

Second, once again, would you rather submit to a heart surgeon who follows a proven process step by step each time he does a particular operation or one who intuitively decides how he's going to attack each operation at the time he dons his surgical gloves? Would you rather fly in a plane with a pilot who goes by the book on every takeoff or one who "wings it" each time he pushes back from the gate?

Knowing and Expanding Your Limits

In medicine, in flying, in golf, it's the knowledge of the processes involved and the skill and experience built up by continuously using them that separates the leaders from the also-rans. The same is true in business, in government, in teaching, in every profession.

Although few executives are computer experts, most recognize that a computer can't effectively process information without the proper software. The thinking processes employed in effective problem solving and decision making are nothing other than software for your brain; they are thoughtware. Just as it takes a lot of diligent, continuing, hands-on practice to become proficient with software such as WordPerfect, Lotus Notes, or PowerPoint, it takes regular use of your cranial decision-making software to develop true thinking skill.

Fortunately for computer users, electronic processors usually beep or fail to comply if an attempt is made to use their software incorrectly. Unfortunately for decision makers, cranial processors have no such built-in safety device. It takes significant openness and objectivity to be able to recognize when the software for the brain isn't up to the task at hand. It takes significant humility to accept it and undertake the work of reprogramming one's own thinking methods.

Part II

THE BASIC TOOLBOX

This section explains the fundamental thinking processes involved in effective problem solving. It opens with Chapter 4 on Situation Assessment, a process for determining the thinking processes that need to be used on the concerns you're facing. The remaining four chapters discuss and illustrate each of these thinking processes at its fundamental level:

Chapter 5 on Decision Analysis—a process for making choices.

Chapter 6 on Implementation Planning—a process for defining the steps and timing involved in making a decision happen.

Chapter 7 on Potential Problem/Opportunity Analysis—a process for detecting and preventing things that could go wrong or detecting good things that could happen.

Chapter 8 on Problem Analysis—a process for finding the cause of things that have unexpectedly changed.

4

Situation Assessment

Situation Assessment is a tool for evaluating all the thinking projects, the unresolved concerns, that are gathering dust on your desk. Its use is akin to spreading the problems out on top of your desk; then dusting each one off and deciding what needs to be done to it—what thinking tool needs to be applied to it; then making sure that no concerns are stuck together; and finally deciding in what order you're going to analyze and resolve them.

The process of Situation Assessment has five steps:

1. Recognize
2. Separate
3. Define Givens
4. Set Priority
5. Select Process

If managers had only one situation of concern staring them in the face at any point, life would be simple. However, the cold hard reality is that most managers have more on their plates at any one time than they can immediately handle. Thus they need to set priorities. But priority setting is one of the last steps in Situation Assessment. Setting priorities for an incomplete list of concerns can have consequences that range from inconsequential to explosive.

Step One: Recognize

The critical first step in "getting your ducks in line" is to be sure that you have identified all the ducks. In other words, you need to recognize all the situations of potential concern. This is where many people drop the ball—it's the old story of out of sight, out of mind. "If I can't see any problems, then there must not be any there."

A major contributor to the magnitude of many problems is that people fail to recognize situations that have the potential to grow into major problems—or opportunities—in their early formative stages. This is the "tip of the iceberg" syndrome. If everything that can be easily seen looks okay, then that which is hidden beneath the surface—what must be pried apart before it can be seen—must be okay as well.

If you mentally go back to the Past/Future, Planned/Unplanned Change model for a moment and think about it, you will probably agree that most of the situations that people miss are of the Unplanned Future Change genre. If a bona-fide problem—an Unplanned Past Change—exists, seldom does it exist undetected. When a decision—a Planned Future Change—needs to be made, seldom are those involved unaware of it. However, all too often people are unaware of the potential disasters, or opportunities, that lie just around the corner.

When it comes to the Recognize step, it's the area of Potential Problems and Potential Opportunities—the Unplanned Future Change—that most often needs serious attention. That's where thinking battles are often won or lost.

And there's another piece to this reality. When you're concerned about problems and decisions, these concerns usually lie within your day-to-day frame of reference, within a defined and confined section of the 360 degrees of your total environment. However, if you really want to think about *all* the potential problems and potential opportunities that could lie ahead, you have to be willing to throw away your daily boundaries and look at the entire 360-degree view of your situations. That is an arduous task that you really may not want to undertake. (But, if you do, a tool that can help is discussed in Chapter 11.)

For the moment, consider the fact that the tools of Potential Problem Analysis and Potential Opportunity Analysis can be used both in a micro as well as a macro perspective. Think of the micro perspective as your day-to-day information base or frame of reference. Think of the macro perspective as your 360-degree environment, your charted and uncharted waters. In this part, we'll deal with the micro uses of these tools. Later, in Part III (The Advanced Toolbox), we'll get into their macro uses.

To recognize situations that might deserve attention, use questions like these:

- What uncertainties, unknowns, exist?
- What questions need to be answered?
- How could things change?
- What is going differently than expected?
- If present trends continue, where could things go?
- What isn't guaranteed, isn't a sure thing?
- What moves could someone else make that could change things?

Notice that these questions are neutral; none of them implies a value judgment, either positive or negative. To become really good at recognizing situations that should be examined, develop your proficiency in using such information-gathering questions as these.

Also, don't overlook how these questions can be used by a team or a group as well. Project teams, new product teams, functional departments, ad hoc committees, and so on can, and should, effectively employ these concepts.

The following questions all imply value judgments. They use words like "bother" and "better"; they tap emotional reactions and personal views and idiosyncratic estimates of worth. Unfortunately, they are ones that people are often more accustomed to asking about situations. Use them if you must, but work hard at displacing them with the preceding questions because the object is not to gauge how you or someone else feels about a situation or whether the situation is better or worse, but whether that situation has a marked potential or need for change.

- What is bothering you?
- What concerns do you have?
- What isn't meeting expectations?
- What's exceeding expectations?
- What could be going better?

After asking your questions, you will have a Recognize list, a complete list—you hope—of the situations that are of concern to you. Your next step is to separate.

Step Two: Separate

Situations should be defined and dealt with at a level that embraces each situation's own unique set of circumstances, conditions, or variables—its own "family" of information. Failure to break a "mess" apart into manageable, discrete segments or pieces typically leads to ineffective or failed problem solving. A converse mistake is to combine several seemingly related concerns into one big catchall, assuming that this will make the problem solving easier. Nothing could be further from the truth. At best the conclusions reached by such combining will be weakened; at worst they'll be totally incorrect.

For some unknown reason, human beings have a tendency to want to agglomerate situations that are of concern to them; in effect they want to create a "mess." Perhaps it's a function of a macho instinct to want to "look at the big picture." The reason is irrelevant. What is relevant is that, in most cases, combining concerns is exactly the wrong thing to do.

Failure to separate accomplishes only one thing—it's a security blanket for the uninitiated and it keeps the problem fuzzy and nebulous. Separating makes the unsolvable solvable. The beauty of keeping things complex is that the buck never lands on anyone's desk; the agony of making things simple is that inept problem solving is traceable.

Managers need to separate problems, decisions, and potential problems. Here are examples of each action.

Separating Problems

Suppose you were faced with a problem—an Unplanned Past Change—of "excessive rejects" of some products and, let's face it, you know what is being rejected and for what reasons:

- Product A is being rejected for poor paint coverage.
- Product Q is being rejected for being too noisy when operated.
- Product W is being rejected for not meeting the tensile strength test.

Most people would clearly see this excessive rejects situation as being three separate and likely independent problems that should be analyzed individually. Most likely, each reject condition has its own, independent cause. Let's dig a little deeper. How do people typically react when a single product has a series of excessive rejects? It turns out that product W has failed the tensile strength test on the 3rd, 10th, 15th, and 26th of the month. Is there one tensile-strength problem or are there four? Many would-be problem solvers' first reaction would be to opt for the former, assuming that the same cause is responsible for all four incidents. However, the bottom line is that it's safer—and often easier—to assume that the causes are different.

After all, once you do a Problem Analysis on one incident and find its true cause, it's very easy to then take your finding and move on to the second incident and see if that cause fits its circumstances. If it does, you're in good shape—you can now move on to the third incident, and so on. However, if it doesn't, you have just become aware of the morass—or mess—you'd be in if you had assumed that the four incidents constituted one tensile-strength problem.

All too often when a problem recurs, when the tensile-strength problem appears for the second time, people jump to the instantaneous conclusion: "It's the same problem as last time." Oh really? If it is, and if you "solved" it the first time around, then you must have done a poor job. Otherwise why would it recur only a week later?

Let's go back to "Product A is being rejected for poor paint coverage" for a minute and use it to illustrate the concept of "stairstepping," a valuable tool in the separate process. Initially, the problem was recognized as excessive rejects (of Product A). However, it was also recognized that the cause of excessive rejects of Product A was known: poor paint coverage.

Graphically, this could be depicted (P = problem, C = cause) as shown in Figure 4.1. At this point, we're left with the question of "What caused the poor paint coverage?" Do we know why the poor paint coverage exists? It turns out that we do; the poor coverage was caused by contaminated air in our paint system. Do we know why the air was contaminated? Yes, we do. Apparently, the maintenance people temporarily switched the paint spray system to another compressed air system—one that had "dirty" air—so that they could make some changes in the regular air system.

P1 = Excessive rejects of Product A

     └→ C1 = P2 = Poor paint coverage

          └→ C2 = ?

Figure 4.1   Stairstep Illustration

Now the stairstepping has produced this new depiction of the situation shown in Figure 4.2. Thus the "problem" has taken on new stripes as a result of asking "Why?" Stairstepping, asking why, is both a valuable and a dangerous tool. It is valuable in that it quickly moves a problem down to the fundamental level that must be dealt with. It is dangerous in that it can be an open invitation to "jump to cause."

All too often, would-be problem solvers assume that they know the true cause—often because of a pet idea—when they do not. Thus they will take stairstepping a step too far, which inevitably results in a problem that does

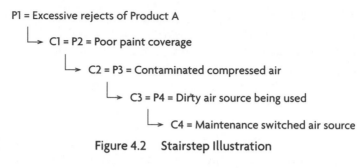

Figure 4.2   Stairstep Illustration

not get solved and therefore often keeps recurring.

Stairstep only to the extent that can be supported by valid information. Stairstep down to the point where uncertainty exists; never go beyond this point—the point at which the problem is ready for Problem Analysis.

Separating Decisions

Suppose you've just accepted a new job in a major metropolitan area that you're completely unfamiliar with. You've already made a decision that you're going to buy a house—there's no uncertainty present here—you're not going to rent or purchase a condo. So the obvious question is "Which house should I buy?"

However, since you're unfamiliar with the area, in reality you have just lumped several decisions together. Because this is a major metropolitan area, it obviously covers a lot of square miles. Within these many square miles are a wide variety of towns, neighborhoods, different standards of living, cultural and social amenities, and so on. To search for "*the* house" within the total area would be an unwieldy task. It's likely that you'll achieve a better outcome more easily by separating the situation into several sequential decisions such as:

- What area do I want to live in?
- What town do I want to live in?
- Which house should I buy?

Notice that the second question is dependent on the first; its range of options will be influenced by the outcome of the initial decision. Likewise, the third question is dependent on the outcome of the second; its range of options will be constrained by the outcome of the second decision. These three decisions also illustrate the concept of stairstepping; each decision is ready for Decision Analysis.

Separating Potential Problems

In a Potential Problem Analysis—Unplanned Future Change—situation, it may also be prudent to break the big picture into smaller situations. Suppose your new job is to head up a new commercial bakery that your employer is building. You might see the need to debug the facility before it's started up and express this need as "Identify the potential problems in the new bakery." However, you'll stand a better chance of finding all the gremlins if you separate your task into functional areas, for example:

- Identify the potential problems in the ingredients handling.
- Identify the potential problems in the mixing operations.
- Identify the potential problems in the baking area.
- Identify the potential problems in the packaging area.

Step Three: Define Givens

Before starting an analysis, particularly a Decision Analysis or a Potential Problem Analysis, it can often be helpful to define any predetermined boundaries or constraints to be imposed on the analysis; these are factors or conditions that are going to be accepted as given. Likewise, in many situations it can be helpful to list the factors behind the perceived need for the analysis, things relating to the status quo that are given and that suggest the need to do something. Sometimes givens are found in, or evolve from, existing company policies; sometimes they establish new policies, either temporary or permanent.

In a Decision Analysis to determine how to rationalize a product line, a marketing executive might choose to impose the following conditions on the outcome:

- The outcome has to be accomplishable within two years without adding any staff.
- The outcome has to be related to our existing products; no new products can be added.

Or, in this same Decision Analysis, the executive might acknowledge that:

- 92% of our business comes from our basic models.
- 79% of our repeat business is for our electrically powered models.

In a Potential Problem Analysis to detect what could go wrong in the manufacture of a new product, a manufacturing executive might choose to impose the following assumptions on the analysis:

- All materials specifications completely and correctly define all the characteristics the materials should possess.
- All purchased materials will be presumed to meet all of our specifications when we receive them.

Or, in this same Potential Problem Analysis, a product development manager might recollect that:

- Of the last four products we've launched, three had to be redesigned within a few months.
- Our last two product launches were delayed for several months by problems in production.

Sometimes a situation doesn't face any significant, relevant givens. However, when they do exist, getting them down in black and white up front can greatly ease and speed up the subsequent analysis.

Often problem solvers are prone to put off thinking about givens until they are ready to analyze a particular concern. However, in many cases, the constraints or factors that underlie the situation, the givens, can have an impact on priority setting.

Step Four: Set Priority

Once you have a list of recognized situations that have been separated out, most likely you're going to have to do some priority setting. Unfortunately, too many people set priorities on a "first come, first served" basis; the first item entered in their date book for a particular time is what gets done. If another issue subsequently arises that must be dealt with at that same time, it's "Tough luck, I'm already scheduled for then." They could care less that the subsequent issue might be more important or have greater urgency.

In effect, setting priorities is really nothing more than making a decision; it is a Decision Analysis process. As such, it can range from a simple evaluation of all your situations against the two objectives of importance and urgency to a more comprehensive, full-blown Decision Analysis discussed in Chapter 10.

Using the two objectives of importance and urgency and judgment calls of high, medium, or low to evaluate the various concerns, you could produce a matrix like that shown in Table 4.1.

Table 4.1. Priority-Setting Matrix

	Importance	*Urgency*
Problem A	L	M
Problem B	H	H
Problem C	M	H
Problem D	M	L
Problem E	H	M

In this sample matrix, Problem B receives the highest priority. It would be followed by either C or E, according to the relationship you establish between importance and urgency. Stephen Covey suggests that you put importance ahead of urgency.[1] Likewise, A and D would be arrayed accordingly.

However, don't overlook the fact that there may be independent/dependent relationships, particularly among decision and potential problem situations, that do their own job of priority setting. The previous house purchase Decision Analyses and the new bakery debugging Potential Problem Analyses illustrate these relationships.

An example of a situation where you need to do a full-blown Decision Analysis—not just a simple importance and urgency matrix—in order to set priorities entails having a myriad of new product ideas on the table but the resources to pursue only a fraction of them. This can be a high-risk, bet-the-company issue in which different people and constituencies are all clamoring for their pet ideas, their babies, to be at the top of the list.

Having been involved in many projects of this "new product priorities" type over the years, in *every* case I observed that the priority order that resulted was not one that any of those who participated in the determination had guessed beforehand. In one instance, a division general manager was so incensed when his pet new product idea wound up at the bottom of the list that he unilaterally moved it to the number one spot. When corporate headquarters heard about this a few months later, they ordered him to drop the project immediately.

Step Five: Select Process

Before talking about selecting the appropriate thinking tool, one qualifier needs to be discussed—"uncertainty." For concerns on your list for which the best way of handling them, the only thing to do, is obvious, there isn't any need to spend time thinking about which process to use for analyzing them. However, before accepting the conclusion that the answers are obvious, pause a moment and reflect on the concerns; make sure no uncertainties are lying under the surface or that you're not really looking at a "tip of the iceberg" situation. For example, going back to the four-level stairstepping shown in the "Excessive rejects of Product A" illustration, do you really know for a fact that each of the causes is true?

By this stage, many problem solvers have already—consciously or subconsciously—decided which thinking process needs to be applied to each of the situations on their lists. Often these choices have been influenced by a mind-set that's focused on a term like "problem" or "decision" or "potential problem," and occasionally these mind-set choices are incorrect. For example, it's always possible that a thinking process mentally locked onto at the Recognize step could be inappropriate given what was uncovered in the Separate step. Do yourself a favor, look at the Past/Future, Planned/Unplanned Change model in Figure 4.3 and let it be your guide.

- If the situation involves an Unplanned Past Change for which you want to determine the cause, you need to use the *Problem Analysis* process (Chapter 8).
- If the situation involves the need to make a Planned Future Change, and you need to decide exactly what that change should be, you need to use the *Decision Analysis* process (Chapter 5).
- If the situation involves the potential for detrimental Unplanned Future Change and you want to identify and prevent such occurrences, you need to use the *Potential Problem Analysis* process (Chapter 7).
- If the situation involves the potential for desirable Unplanned Future Change and you want to identify and promote such occurrences, you need to use the *Potential Opportunity Analysis* process (Chapter 11).

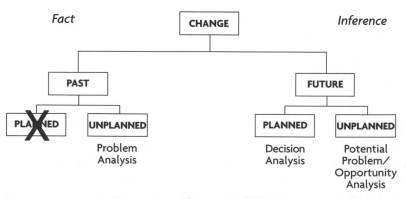

Figure 4.3   Change Model No. 3

That, in a nutshell, is what Situation Assessment is all about.

To illustrate a number of the steps discussed in this and the following chapters, I provide examples of meetings held to determine the location for a new regional headquarters. Here the team members are performing Situation Assessment.

The Meeting

Although the process of Situation Assessment consists of five steps (Recognize, Separate, Define Givens, Set Priority, and Select Process), in many problem-solving meetings not all of these steps are required. In some, the situation as it's posed is all ready for a particular type of analysis. Thus the meeting leader must decide which, if any, of the Situation Assessment steps are required and proceed accordingly.

For example, in the illustration in which you've just been hired to head up a new commercial bakery, if your new boss has told you that your number one priority is to make sure it runs like a Swiss watch from day one, the Set Priority step has been done for you.

Occasionally a meeting leader will be asked to help on a problem that the person who "owns" the problem can't really articulate. The person with the concern will vacillate, uttering vague comments like "Things aren't going right," or "I don't think we're on top of this," or "I think we need to be doing things differently." The first step of Situation Assessment, recognize, can help here.

Many problems proposed for resolution in meetings are unsolvable as initially stated. They're a "can of worms." They are, in effect, a collection of discrete, individual problems that haven't been seen as such. They have been perceived as one big, fuzzy, mass—or mess—that no one can seem to grasp. The Separate step dissects and recasts unsolvable messes into separate, solvable problems.

If a problem-solving group is faced with a lengthy list of problems that need to be resolved, in some way this list is going to have to be put into a priority order. This order may be based on the relative importance of the independent problems or on independent/dependent relationships among them. Whichever the case, the Set Priority step accomplishes this.

Step One: Recognize

In most cases when people are asked to conduct meetings, the Recognize step has already been accomplished. A meeting leader is asked to:

"Help us solve the problem of _____"
or
"We need help deciding _____."

However, there are occasions when the person asking for help is at the can-of-worms, mess level. Let's assume that is the case in this example. The feeling is that "This is the first time we've ever thought about setting up a regional office and we just don't know where to begin." To open up people's minds, the leader might start the Situation Assessment meeting by asking:

"Why do we need a regional office at all?"
or
"What are the things that are bothering you about setting up a regional office, what are the questions that you think need to be answered, what concerns do you have?"

As the responses to these questions start to pour out, it is important to get every input listed as quickly as possible so none are lost. There is no need to polish the wording at this point. The leader prodded the group with a variety of exploratory questions until the well ran dry. The team members produced a list that included these issues:

1. Where should we put the regional office?
2. Who should staff it?
3. What functions should be handled in a regional office?
4. We don't have it in the budget.

The first three items expressed uncertainty—they stated questions that needed to be answered. However, the fourth item, "We don't have it in the budget," was simply a statement of fact; although it expressed a concern, it didn't express an uncertainty. So the leader probed this item and converted it into questions to be answered:

• How much can we afford to spend to get the regional office set up?

• Should we spread it over this and next year's budgets?

At this point, it looked like the well was dry. It was time to move on to the next step. But the leader remained aware that any step in any process could and should be revisited whenever new, or overlooked, relevant information might come up. If at a later point a participant thought of a previously unrecognized concern and uncertainty, the leader would go back and add it to the Recognize list.

Step Two: Separate

The first uncertainty on the list, "Where should we put it?" could be interpreted in many different ways. The question as written could be subject to many possibilities. To one participant it might mean: "In what part of the country should we locate it?" To another, it might mean: "Should we place it downtown or near the airport?"

When the team members separated this macro question out, they produced this list of individual uncertainties:

> Should we place it downtown or near the airport?
> Which city should we put it in?
> What part of the country should we put it in?
> Should we locate it in a major city or a smaller one?

Then the meeting leader examined every concern on the Recognize list to make sure each expressed a single, stand-alone, question. One way to determine this is to say,

> "If I asked different people what the possible scope of answers to this question could be, might I get different answers?"

If the answer is yes, there's a need to separate more. Another way to determine this is to say,

> "If we analyze this problem as it's presently stated, exactly what specific things could be affected by the outcome?"

If asking this question yields two or more unrelated answers, go back and separate some more.

Step Three: Define Givens

Recognizing that this new regional office will be a first, the meeting leader wanted to probe the group to uncover any conditions or factors that should guide later choices about the office. Most of the questions the group has identified thus far relate to the regional office's location, and in discussing the situation the problem solvers didn't see any givens relative to that location. However, the group quickly recognized that this would be the first time the company had ever asked employees to relocate. After considerable discussion, they concluded that:

> We will use this new location to promote/upgrade as many of our employees as possible.

All moves will be strictly voluntary; no pressure of any kind will be put on any employee to relocate.

Whether they realized it or not, the problem solvers had established new company policy with these givens. Also, although these givens weren't relevant to the decision questions on the present list, it was obvious that they would come into play in subsequent decisions in the future and thus the meeting leader held them in reserve for that time.

Step Four: Set Priority

Some of the questions that a team recognizes and separates out may be interrelated. And even those that stand alone will still be subject to that old bit of wisdom, "We can't do everything at once." Thus, before the individual concerns can be tackled, the problem solvers must set priorities. They must decide the order in which the issues should be attacked.

Looking at the four location decisions, the team members in this case decided that the decisions need to be resolved in the following sequence:

D1 = What part of the country should we put it in?
D2 = Should we locate it in a major city or a smaller one?
D3 = Which city should we put it in?
D4 = Should we place it downtown or near the airport?

What the problem solvers said by constructing this sequence was that D1 was the independent decision. How they proceeded in D2 would depend on the outcome of D1. Likewise, the makeup of the D3 analysis would depend on the outcome of D2, and D4 would be influenced by D3.

As they examined this priority order, one participant commented, "As far as what part of the country we should put it in, the answer is obvious. It has to be in the southwest. That's the whole reason we got into this predicament; our business in the southwest is booming and we're not handling it well." Because all the participants agreed, the leader crossed that concern off the list. What the problem solvers had said in effect was: "There's no uncertainty about that question, we know the answer."

Another participant observed, "We don't need to separate out the second and third questions. When we decide the city, we can factor in the characteristics that relate to city size." The rest agreed that these concerns could easily be handled that way.

So by looking for obvious answers and combining concerns that do not need to be separate, the team members boiled the location questions and their priorities down to:

D1 = Which city should we put it in?

D2 = Should we place it downtown or near the airport?

Going back to the initial Recognize list, the remaining questions still had to be prioritized:

• Who should staff it?

• What functions should be handled in a regional office?

The problem solvers might have seen these concerns as independent of the location questions. But, on closer examination, they recognized that some people might refuse a transfer to a major metropolitan area while others might not want to relocate to anything but a big city. Thus, "Who should staff it?" could wind up in the sequence.

"Wait a minute," someone said, "wouldn't it be prudent to know what functions are going to be placed in the regional office before we decide whom to transfer there? After all, what we're going to do there could influence how it is staffed." Thus the final priority sequence was:

D1 = Which city should we put it in?

D2 = Should we place it downtown or near the airport?

D3 = What functions should be handled in a regional office?

D4 = Who should staff it?

The point is that no individual or organization can do everything at once. Time and resources must be allocated; that is what priority setting is all about. Before tackling any situation, problem solvers should have a plan of attack that defines in what order they will work on each individual issue.

Whether it is determined by examining the independent/dependent relationships among the individual issues or, if they're all independent of each other, by assessing the relative importance and urgency of each, the priority sequence is the master plan for problem-solving resource allocation.

Step Five: Select Process

Considering all the discussion that they've had about D1, D2, D3, and D4, the team agreed that all the concerns related to Planned Future Change; thus they all called for the Decision Analysis process.

In Summary: Situation Assessment

The concepts of Situation Assessment are:

1. Recognize
   - What is bothering you?
   - What questions need to be answered?
   - What concerns do you have?
   - What uncertainties exist?
   - Concern + uncertainty = problem

2. Separate
   - Single area involved
   - Single family of options

3. Define Givens
   - Identify boundaries/constraints
   - Know why you need to analyze this

4. Set Priority
   - Identify independent/dependent relationships
   - Determine relative importance/urgency

5. Select Process
   - Unplanned Past Change = Problem Analysis
   - Planned Future Change = Decision Analysis
   - Unplanned Future Change = Potential Problem/Opportunity Analysis

5

Decision Analysis

Most managers spend more of their time dealing with situations in the area of future change—"What functions should be handled in a regional office?" or "Identify potential problems in the packaging area"—than with situations in the area of past change—"Excessive rejects of Product A." Also, the future-change thinking processes are easier to learn and more forgiving than the past-change process. Within future change, managers tend to be more concerned with the planned than the unplanned (although whether this is prudent is a valid question that we will discuss later). For these reasons, it seems appropriate to start our excursion into the realm of structured thinking with the tools of Planned Future Change—that is, the tools of Decision Analysis (Figure 5.1).

As depicted in the figure, the Decision Analysis process involves five conceptual steps:

1. Define the Decision Statement
2. Establish Objectives
3. Value Objectives
4. Generate Alternatives
5. Compare and Choose

This chapter discusses the procedures and purposes of each step and shows what each step looks like in the example of choosing the location for a new regional headquarters.

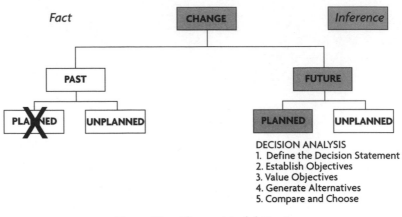

Figure 5.1   Change Model No. 4

Step One: Define the Decision Statement

There are two elements to consider in defining a Decision Statement—its purpose and its level. With regard to purpose, recall the old adage of "A problem properly stated is half solved." The wording of the Decision Statement is *the* key determiner of whether you will breeze through a Decision Analysis or will continuously be bumping into obstacles and making wrong turns. Don't forget:

Each step builds on, evolves from, depends on, the information developed in the preceding steps.

The Decision Statement ultimately defines and controls every subsequent step in the Decision Analysis process.

Purpose

A Decision Statement should start with a verb such as "select," "determine," or "develop." The choice of which of these three words to use can be important because it can have a subtle yet significant impact on the process. Each of these verbs reflects a different mode of Decision Analysis as determined by the alternative(s) that will ultimately be dealt with. Let's examine some explanation for choosing the verb.

Select Mode

"Select" is the best word to use when the alternatives you'll be evaluating are mutually exclusive; that is, you'll be selecting one and, in doing so, eliminating all the others. For example, you're only going to hire one vice president of human resources. Therefore, when you decide to offer the job to Candidate C, you automatically eliminate the other candidates. Of course, if Candidate C doesn't accept your offer, you have the option of falling back to the next best candidate. In this mode, the alternatives are usually standard, or fixed, or off-the-shelf options; they are readily and singularly identifiable. Typical examples of a select mode Decision Statement would be:

- Select the best advertising agency.
- Select the optimum town in which to locate our new plant.
- Select the best vice president of human resources.

Determine Mode

"Determine" is the best word to use when the alternatives are not necessarily mutually exclusive; that is, the alternative ultimately chosen may wind up being a combination or composite of the alternatives analyzed in a first evaluation. In this mode, the alternatives are usually representatives of types or families of options, they are not necessarily individually or rigidly defined. Moreover, in this mode, the Decision Analysis often goes through several evaluations. Once a first cut has been made, the decision maker may step back, examine the results, explore why different options came out better than others, and then look for ways to combine variations of the highly rated alternatives into new combinations, new alternatives, that are then analyzed in a second evaluation. Typical examples of this kind of Decision Statement are:

- Determine the best way(s) to restructure our sales force.
- Determine the optimum way(s) to allocate the manufacture of Product X among our plants.
- Determine the best way(s) to reduce overhead.

Note that these examples state "Determine the best *way(s)....*" This suggests that there may be more than one equally good way of accomplishing this end and it reflects the concept of multiple evaluations. In decisions in which you aren't necessarily limited to one singular option, using the term "way(s)" can serve as an ongoing reminder of this possibility.

Develop Mode

"Develop" is the best word to use when there aren't any existing alternatives from which to make a choice. Thus the Decision Analysis process will be used to design and create the Alternative to be pursued. Typical examples of this Decision Statement are:

- Develop the optimum design for Product X.
- Develop the best sales compensation plan.
- Develop the optimum warranty policy.

The term "*the* alternative" is in the singular because there will be only one Product X. True, you may eventually develop a Product Y and a Product Z, but each of these is a product or a design unto itself. Although they may borrow ideas from Product X, designing each is a separate undertaking.

Changing a Mode

Occasionally, you may end up changing the mode of a decision. For example, suppose that your Decision Statement is "Select the best house to buy." The implication here is that you're out to buy a house that already exists. However, suppose that after weeks of arduous looking, you arrive at the conclusion that nothing on the market comes close to meeting your objectives. You could take the *same* set of objectives that you established and give them to an architect. However, you don't want to pay the architect to come up with ten designs and then "Select the best house to build." So you change the Decision Statement to "Develop the best new house" and ask the architect to use the *same* set of objectives to design *the* optimum alternative.

Seek the Best

Your Decision Statement should always include the word "best" or "optimum." The purist may suggest that the optimum is never attainable, that it's always over the next hill. Conceptually, this is true: however, it's also an absurdity for this purpose. The value in having best or optimum in the Decision Statement is that you are continually reminded that you're not looking for just any old answer, you're out to find the answer that surpasses all the others you can think of.

KISS

After you have chosen a decision mode and have written down "Determine the best _____" (or whatever you have picked), you then need to simply and succinctly complete the statement describing the choice to be made. As you have seen in the previous examples, Keep It Short and Simple!

An all-too-common trap in creating a Decision Statement is that people want to stretch the statement out so that it severely constrains the scope of the options. For example, "Determine the best way(s) to restructure our sales force that won't increase our staffing level or require relocating many people." All this detail impinges on the step that follows, that of establishing objectives, and runs the serious risk of skewing the analysis. Remember the KISS dictum: Keep It Short and Simple. Simply express the *net effect* that you're out to accomplish. We will explore this more later in the chapter.

The (So-called) Binary Decision

What about the situation in which you're faced with only two options—yes or no. How do you handle a decision like that? The blunt answer is, you don't; at best there's a 50/50 chance of disaster. Why? Because no matter how you look at a (presumed) yes/no decision, you're not looking at the *true choice*, the *net effect*. It's virtually impossible to derive an unbiased set of objectives from a Decision Statement with stated or implied yes or no alternatives.

Suppose the CEO of a major competitor, XYZ Industries, called you, the CEO of ABC Corporation, and told you he was thinking of selling XYZ and wanted to give you the first crack. An instantaneous reflex reaction might be to frame the question as "Should we buy XYZ?"—a decision with the obvious alternatives: yes or no.

But attempting to derive and define objectives from a Decision Statement like "Should we buy XYZ?" will lead to a stacked deck—one leaning toward "yes" or "no"—based on your conscious or subconscious biases, emotions, and so on. If you step back and reflect on the situation for a moment, you will recognize that whether you acquire XYZ or don't, you will have influenced the future course of ABC. Thus the true choice you're facing, the net effect, is "Determine the optimum future path for ABC."

Notice also that this Decision Statement has been cast in the determine mode rather than the select mode. It may appear at first that the alternatives are:

1. Continue ABC as we are presently structured.
2. Combine XYZ with ABC.

But when you apply a little thought to such binary situations, in many cases there are more options available than the assumed yes/no equivalents. In this example, there are probably several other alternatives such as:

3. Combine XYZ with ABC and then sell off their Motors Division.
4. Combine XYZ with ABC and then acquire a related distribution organization.
5. ?

When it's all over and the dust has settled, you either will have accepted XYZ's offer or you won't. But, most important, you will have made that choice based on the net effect, "the optimum future path for ABC."

Whenever a decision situation appears to offer only yes/no alternatives, recognize that it doesn't express the true choice. Recast it to reflect the net effect.

Level

Once you have focused the Decision Statement so that it accurately reflects the purpose of the decision, you must consider one more point: Does the Decision Statement cut in at—does it describe—the appropriate level of decision, the desired net effect? Often decisions that relate to a choice made previously are jumped into with the assumption that the new decision should be undertaken at the same level as the previous one. For example, several years ago you decided which company to buy component Z from. Since that company is now going out of business, you need to select a new vendor—or do you?

In the past, the Decision Statement may have been something like "Select the best vendor for component Z." Perhaps now, because of changing circumstances, you should move the decision up a level to "Select the best way to obtain component Z," which would enable you to consider making it internally as well as buying it outside.

Or perhaps, due to your company's rapid growth and geographic diversity, more and more of its top executives are spending more time sitting around airports waiting for connecting flights just to attend an hour-long meeting. The chairman has decided to bring this waste of time to a screeching halt by buying a corporate jet. The task assigned to you: "Select the best corporate jet to buy." But is this really the true choice—is it actually the best way of accomplishing the net effect?

Isn't the desired net effect to dramatically reduce the time spent getting to and from diverse locations? Then why not move the Decision Statement up a level to something like "Determine the best way(s) to provide for our executives' remote transportation needs." Here the alternatives would be broader in scope; this is where you'll find out if owning your own corporate jet is the best alternative. At this higher level of decision, the alternatives could include buying your own jet, chartering aircraft when needed, joint ownership of a corporate aircraft with another company, and so forth.

It might even be desirable to move the Decision Statement up even another level to something like "Determine the best way(s) for our top executives to be in effective communication with our distant or remote locations." In this case, the alternatives could include installing a video communication system, subscribing to a commercial video conferencing service, arranging for available-on-demand aircraft, and so on.

The point is simple: Make sure your Decision Statement is cast at the appropriate and highest level that responds to the net effect you're out to achieve. The key is to ask yourself: Is the answer to the *preceding* level decision known or is it really an assumption that should be reexamined? The risk in determining the level is that the decision makers will cut in at too low a level. The risk of cutting in too high is essentially nonexistent. Why? Because the worst that will happen at the higher level is that effort will be devoted to a decision that doesn't need to be made, one whose answer is already known. Invariably this will become blatantly obvious to the decision maker early on before too much time is invested in the effort. At the lower level, however, the risk is an outcome that is far from optimum.

The Meeting

In the previous chapter on Situation Assessment, the problem-solving team assigned to determine the location of a new regional headquarters produced a list of four decisions that needed to be resolved and put them in this priority sequence:

D1 = Which city should we put it in?
D2 = Should we place it downtown or near the airport?
D3 = What functions should be handled in a regional office?
D4 = Who should staff it?

They also determined that a Decision Analysis wasn't necessary at the level preceding what is now D1 (What part of the country . . . ?) because that answer was obvious; there was no uncertainty present.

In light of their discussion about the fundamentals of Decision Statements, the team members recast their wording of these statements:

D1 = Select the best city for our southwest regional office.
D2 = Select the best part/area of the city for our office.
D3 = Determine what functions should be handled in a regional office.
D4 = Determine who we should move to our southwest regional office.

No sooner had this been done than one participant piped up with: "There's one question we forgot—we don't have it in the budget. Should we spread it over this and next year's budgets? How does that fit into select, determine, develop?" It was obvious that this represented a yes/no question that had to be recast. "Should we spread it over this and next year's budgets?" didn't state the true choice they were facing. The true choice, the net effect that needed to be decided, was "Determine the optimum time frame for absorbing these (regional office setup) costs." From this Decision Statement they could readily and easily establish objectives that delineate exactly what an optimum time frame should be. In this scenario, they listed these alternatives among others:

- Absorb all the costs this year.
- Split them 50%/50% between this year and next.
- Split them 33%/67% between this year and next.
- Push them all into next year.

The group then concluded that the "time frame for absorbing costs" decision didn't have any linkage to their D1 to D4 priority order. They gave it the label of D? and referred it to the vice president of finance for resolution.

Step Two: Establish Objectives

The second step in Decision Analysis is to define the objectives that will be used to control the selection of the alternative. The whole function of the Decision Statement is to provide a springboard, a focal point, for establishing objectives which define the specific, individual criteria that will be used to evaluate the alternatives being considered.

If the Decision Analysis you're working on came about because of shortcomings in the present way of doing something, because of weaknesses in an existing alternative, it can be helpful to create a list of the concerns about the present circumstances—the givens—before beginning to establish objectives. This helps ensure that the completed set of objectives speaks to all these concerns.

The term "objectives" ranks high on the list of all-time favorite business buzz words and can mean different things to different people. In Decision Analysis,

> An objective is a specific, singular description of a desired *result* or output to be achieved or avoided, or a desired *resource* or input to be used or avoided.

Recall that Decision Statements always include the word "best" or "optimum" (select the *best* vice president of human resources; determine the *best* way(s) to restructure our sales force; develop the *optimum* warranty policy).

Objectives serve to define exactly and comprehensively what constitutes *optimum* or *best* in the decision maker's eyes; objectives should consider 360 degrees of the *system* embraced by the decision and surrounding and impinging on it. For example, the system impinging on the decision to "Determine the best way(s) to restructure our sales force" might include:

Accounting	Order processing
Advertising	Order scheduling
Car leasing	Sales force
Competitors	Sales management
Credit department	Sales offices
Customers	Sales support
Distributors	Travel department
Marketing	

The relevant scope of the system encompassed by a decision can be defined as including anything—any area, any element—that has the potential of influencing the success or effectiveness of the results you're out to achieve—regardless of whether you have the ability to influence the area or element.

Results and Resources

To establish objectives, the decision maker needs to direct two questions to the Decision Statement:

1. What *results* or *outputs* do we want to achieve/to avoid in the area of _____?
2. What *resources* or *inputs* do we want to use/to avoid in the area of _____?

These questions will have multiple answers because, when establishing objectives, it is critical that the most comprehensive list possible of results and resources is developed. To maximize the probability that all 360 degrees of the system, all of its areas, will be considered when establishing objectives, use a checklist of trigger words, of thought provokers found in the Objective-Setting Checklist.

The list shown here is only one example of such a checklist. People whose decisions often relate to specific functional areas or specific business areas might find it helpful to construct their own specialized checklists. A human resources executive's list might be very different from a purchasing executive's; a healthcare industry executive's list might be very different from a computer industry executive's list.

OBJECTIVE-SETTING CHECKLIST

ECONOMY
Controls
Cycles
Inflation
Interrelationships
Limitations
Size
Trends

ENVIRONMENT
Appearance
Climate
Crime
Culture
Ecology
Legal
Natural disaster
Political
Pollution
Regulatory
Religious
Social

EQUIPMENT/FACILITIES
Accessibility
Adaptability
Capabilities
Efficiency
Interdependence
Life
Location
Replacement
Security
Size
Storage
Tolerances
Utilization
Yield

FINANCIAL/MONEY
Availability
Capital
Costs
Exchange rates
Fixed
Liability
Long/short term
Return
Risk
Sources
Uses
Variable

MARKETPLACE
Competition
Demand
Demography
Distribution
Elasticity
Geography
Image
Market share
Opportunities
Position
Promotion
Regulation
Risks
Seasonality
Segments
Trade barriers
Trends

MATERIALS
Availability
Configuration
Costs
Disposal
Energy
Hazardous
Natural resources
Quality
Scarcity
Sources
Substitutes

METHODS/TECHNOLOGY
Adaptability
By-products
Innovation
Obsolescence
Patentability
Procedures
Proprietary
Repeatability
Tolerances
Security
Waste

ORGANIZATION/PEOPLE
Adaptability
Attitudes
Communication
Compatibility
Conflict
Coordination
Development
Flexibility
Groups
Health
Interests
Interrelationships
Knowledge
Mobility
Motivation
Opportunities
Performance
Productivity
Responsibilities
Safety
Skills
Strengths
Weaknesses

PRODUCT/SERVICE
Appearance
Complexity
Gaps
Liability
Life cycle
Maintenance
Performance
Pricing
Proliferation
Quality
Repair
Simplicity
Size
Strengths
Warranty
Weaknesses
Weight

TIME
Cycles
Deadlines
Maximum
Minimum
Periods

Applying the sample checklist to the "Determine the best way(s) to restructure our sales force" Decision Statement, one might look at the first category, the ECONOMY, and say, "Yes, this decision should consider economic factors." Perusing the trigger words under that heading, one might be grabbed by the word "cycles." This could suggest an objective along the lines of:

- Minimum susceptibility to economic swings.

Thinking further along these lines might produce further objectives, such as:

- Minimum fixed costs.
- Maximum ability to easily scale the organization up or down.

And don't limit yourself only to the trigger words in the list. It is simply a representative memory jogger and as such will never be complete; anything relative to the economy that comes to mind is fair game. Moving on to the second category, the ENVIRONMENT, the trigger word "legal" might suggest an objective like:

- Minimum potential for illegal or unethical actions or relationships.

Each category, and its trigger words, should be explored for potential objectives. Some representative objectives that might be triggered along the way include:

- Maximum ability to be ahead of the competition.
- Maximum ability to serve evolving market niches.
- Can be fully implemented in one year.
- Minimize time from order taking through order processing.
- Minimum cost to operate.
- Maximum potential to develop our people.

Notice that almost every objective starts with the words "maximum/ maximize" or "minimum/minimize." This flows from the word "optimize" in the Decision Statement—to optimize is to get as much as possible and give as little as possible.

Occasionally problem solvers will disagree over an objective. For example, if the objective is "Can be fully implemented in one year," one person might feel that the project should be done much sooner; another might look at it from the perspective of what's the hurry—it's no big deal if it takes a couple of years. To resolve such disagreement, recognize that, in effect:

Every objective is the optimum alternative of the preceding level decision (whether or not that decision was formally made).

In other words, such a disagreement can be resolved by moving to the preceding level decision, which, in this case, would be "Select the optimum implementation period."

Single Variable

When defining objectives, it's important that each objective focus on a single variable. Suppose some decision makers had combined these two objectives:

1. Maximum ability to be ahead of the competition.

and

2. Maximum potential to develop our people.

into one objective

Maximum ability to be ahead of the competition and develop our people.

When it comes time to evaluate the alternatives against such a compound objective, the decision makers will find themselves in great difficulty as they try to evaluate a varying array of contrasting information; it will become an unworkable task. So the rule of the game is for each objective to focus on—measure the satisfaction of—only one variable.

An easy test of the "quality" of the wording of objectives is to show them to someone who wasn't involved in defining them. A complete stranger should be able to understand the concern expressed by each without any additional explanation.

Conflict and Contradiction

As the Establish Objectives step moves on and the list of important considerations gets fleshed out, sooner or later a bolt of lightning will hit. It will be noticed that some objectives are in conflict and that they contradict each other. Of course! What would you expect? When you go to buy a house, you want the most house for the least money. These two objectives are in opposition and that's the way it should be; they each reflect a desired outcome. The satisfaction of opposing objectives is the whole rationale behind this tool called Decision Analysis; it's the beauty of the process. When you use it, your ultimate choice of a home will reflect a balance between size and cost.

The Meeting

Working with the Decision Statement "Select the best city for our southwest regional office," the team members scanned the checklist category headings: ECONOMY, ENVIRONMENT, EQUIPMENT/FACILITIES, and so on, to see if they felt the decision should be influenced by objectives in any of these areas. "Yes, the economy should definitely be considered. What results or outputs do we want to achieve or to avoid in the area of the economy is definitely a question we need to explore."

They then went on to look at the trigger words within the ECONOMY category: "controls," "cycles," "inflation," and so on. "Yes, cycles should definitely be considered," they said, and they established this objective:

  • Has a stable local economy, not subject to wild gyrations.

The trigger word "interrelationships" suggested the objective:

  • Has a broad-based economy, not heavily linked to one industry.

And the trigger word "size" suggested the objectives:

  • Moderate size area.
  • Moderate cost of living.

As is typical, the team members found that the question, "What results . . . ?" was the one that helped them the most. The second question, "What resources . . . ?" usually helps people to uncover only a few objectives, ones affected by resource constraints such as: "Not require more than $200,000 project cost."

Establishing a comprehensive set of objectives is a critical element. Before leaving this step, the leader encouraged the decision-making team to take one more mental trip through the checklist of trigger words to make sure nothing had been overlooked. (If at a later point in the process an overlooked objective is discovered, the team will add it to the list.)

The meeting concluded with the following list of objectives:

  • Excellent air transportation access.
  • Good aesthetic "quality of life" (cultural, educational, etc.).
  • Good office space availability.
  • Good office worker availability.
  • Good physical "quality of life" (general environment).

- Has a broad-based economy, not heavily linked to one industry.
- Has a stable local economy, not subject to wild gyrations.
- Has adequate road infrastructure (easy commuting).
- Moderate cost of living.
- Moderate size area (population).

Notice that they also added parenthetical clarifications to some objectives to make sure that their concerns—the variables they were out to measure—weren't misunderstood. Notice also that "Not require more than $200,000 project cost" wasn't included; we will discuss the reason for that later.

Step Three: Value Objectives

Although all the objectives that have been listed are there because it's felt that they should influence the outcome of the decision, most likely it's also believed that some should have stronger influence than others. If so, then some relative importance should be assigned to each. Detailed explanations of the two ways to value objectives, musts and wants, follow.

Using Must Objectives

There is a school of thought that says that some objectives may be so critical, so important, that an alternative's failure to meet any one of them should be grounds for instant rejection. This school refers to such objectives as musts. In my experience, in most—not all—cases, musts are, at best, a cop out to make life easier for the decision maker; at worst, they can be extremely dangerous.

For example, suppose a company is looking for a new vice president of R&D. Someone might suggest an objective like "Must have an M.B.A. and a Ph.D. in chemistry." Think about it for a minute—do you honestly believe there is no one in the world lacking these two sheepskins who could do an outstanding job of running R&D? "Must have an M.B.A. and a Ph.D. in chemistry" does only one thing, it makes life easier for the person who has to sort through the resumes; it does not guarantee that you'll get the best person to head R&D.

Suppose you're working on a new pricing policy and corporate counsel has decreed that it "Must be legal." Sounds reasonable, but what does that mean in today's world of obtuse, entangling, and sometimes conflicting regulations? Using such an objective as a must to scuttle alternatives at the outset will likely mean that weeks or months will be spent to get beyond that point. A more practical approach might be to ignore the objective at the outset, come up with the best alternative(s), and then give it/them to the lawyers to examine for flaws.

Suppose you're in charge of a major capital expansion project and the CEO has decreed that its cost "Must not exceed $50,000,000." Suppose you find that you could build a facility that would be 15% less costly to operate if you had $10,000 more to spend (a .02% increase). Most prudent project managers would go to the CEO and explain the situation, and most prudent CEOs would instantly come up with the extra funds. So much for the validity of "Must not exceed $50,000,000." Such an objective is truly a must *only* if spending one more dollar would break the company.

Anytime a true must exists, more than likely the objectives list should include a corresponding weighted objective. If $50,000,000 is the absolute spending cap, it's possible that the less costly an alternative is, the more desirable it would be. Thus the list of objectives should probably include an objective like "Minimum cost," which would be used to show that the lower its cost, the more desirable an alternative would be—*if* that is true.

One important point about must objectives—if an objective really is a must and if failure to meet it will definitely spell disaster, then the objective's limit must be precisely defined so that there's no chance of its being interpreted in different ways by different people.

Overall, must objectives seldom improve the quality of the choice. They may improve the speed with which it is made and they may make the analysis easier, but not necessarily better.

Using Want Objectives

Objectives that haven't been labeled as musts are, by definition, wants. Within a decision's spectrum of want objectives, there is usually a wide range of relative importance that needs to be reflected in how they are valued. An effective way of accomplishing this is to use a numerical weighting scale. Much research has determined that the thinnest most people can slice subjective judgments is into 10% increments. Therefore, the largest practical scale would range from 10 to 1.

Recognize that we're talking about *weighting, not ranking*. Ranking says that no two objectives can be equal and that all objectives have an equal differential between them. Weighting says that any objective can occupy any position in a relative scale and that several can be of equal importance. Weighting is much more practical for the decision-making process, as the rest of this chapter will illustrate.

The easiest way to use a 10 to 1 weighting scale is to look at the list and pick out the objective, or objectives, that are of top importance and assign it, or them, a weight of 10. You have now defined the scale. An objective that is two-thirds as important as a 10-weighted objective is assigned a weight of 7, ones that are half as important are assigned a weight of 5, and so on, through the list. Again, since this is a weighting process, there can be several 10's, 9's, 8's, and so on.

Using a 10 to 1 scale also offers an important exclusionary benefit; any objective that isn't worth at least a weight of 1 automatically gets dropped as being a waste of time.

The Meeting

The new regional office team looked at the list of objectives established and unanimously zeroed in on "Moderate cost of living" as the most important objective on the list. This was heavily influenced by the fact that it is what they are accustomed to in their present headquarters city and, given that several people would be moved from this location to the new regional office, they didn't want to disrupt the economics of their lifestyles.

Further discussion led to their deciding that "Moderate size area" and "Has adequate road infrastructure" were also 10's. Continuing discussion resulted in the following list of weights:

10 Moderate size area (population).
10 Moderate cost of living.
10 Has adequate road infrastructure (easy commuting).
 9 Excellent air transportation access.
 8 Good physical "quality of life" (general environment).
 8 Good aesthetic "quality of life" (cultural, educational, etc.).
 7 Has a stable local economy, not subject to wild gyrations.
 7 Good office worker availability.
 5 Good office space availability.
 5 Has a broad-based economy, not heavily linked to one industry.

Step Four: Generate Alternatives

If the decision makers have done their job, they should now have a comprehensive set of objectives that, in effect, define the utopian answer to their quest. Now comes the real-world task of seeing how close they can come to satisfying this utopian set of conditions.

Now, and only now, is it appropriate to start thinking about the alternatives that should be considered in making the decision. But let's be realistic—in many select and determine mode decisions, many of the likely alternatives become obvious as soon as the Decision Statement is nailed down. However, while they were establishing objectives, decision makers should have done everything possible to suppress any thoughts about alternatives.

Why? Because the more you allow thoughts about alternatives to mix and mesh with those about objectives, the more you run the risk of constructing a set of objectives that—whether you intended it or not—favors pet alternatives or those you're more familiar with.

Back in the Decision Statement step, we discussed the three different verbs—select, determine, develop—that are used at the start of the statements and also tie in to modes of generating alternatives.

Select Mode

The word "select" is the one used when the decision involves choosing from among off-the-shelf, mutually exclusive alternatives. For example, if you're out to buy a new car, a new copying machine, a new pair of shoes, a new corporate jet, or whatever—if someone is out to select a college to attend, decide which flight to take, decide the location for a new regional office, or choose which heart surgeon to submit to—in all likelihood these choices will be made from regularly available alternatives. In such situations, there's not a lot that can be said about generating alternatives other than cautioning decision makers to be sure they have thoroughly scanned all the shelves so as not to overlook any newcomers to the scene.

Generating alternatives in the select mode is usually easy. In most cases, the available options are either well known or the ways to identify them are obvious. In the rare circumstance when this is not the case, there are many ways of locating them, such as talking with associates, vendors, customers; exploring on-line data bases; and so on.

Determine Mode

In effect, the determine mode occupies the middle ground between the select and develop modes; it is a synthesis mode. Usually, decision makers will start out considering a range of options. These typically are not of the fixed, off-the-shelf variety, but are readily and easily recognized and defined as a representative cross section of reasonable potential solutions. Generating alternatives in the determine mode should be done cautiously because there are often dozens, if not hundreds, of minute variations of the various options. As mentioned, in most cases such an analysis will proceed through several evaluations.

For example, take the "Determine the best way(s) to restructure our sales force" decision. For starters, there are several "families" of alternatives, such as by:

- Product type
- Geography
- Customer type
- Customer size

However, there also are often a myriad of specific variations within any one of these families. The best way of handling such a situation is to define representative alternatives that constitute middle-of-the-road members of each family and then proceed through a first evaluation of the analysis. Once the outcome is known, you can then use what you've learned to fine-tune variations and combinations of the highly rated alternatives and proceed with a second evaluation. We will delve more into this later in the Compare and Choose section.

The term brainstorming is a widely recognized, as well as a widely abused and misused term. It's a technique that is frequently portrayed as a panacea for problem solving. Brainstorming is *not* a tool for problem solving; it is a tool that can be used *within* the process of problem solving, specifically within the Decision Analysis process. It is a tool for generating alternatives. It can be useful for this when you are in the determine mode.

One final point on selecting or determining alternatives: If the decision you're working on relates to changing something that presently exists—such as an organization structure, a vendor, an advertising agency—*always* include the existing "something" as an alternative in the analysis. By doing so, you will get a relative picture of how the other alternatives compare to what you have now; you might even occasionally be surprised to find out that the existing alternative comes out on top.

Including the existing alternative in your analysis can raise a question about some Decision Statements. For example, in "Determine the best way(s) to *restructure* our sales force," the word "restructure" implies that the decision makers *know* that the existing alternative isn't any good, that it will be bested by at least one other alternative. Isn't this a dangerous assumption? The net effect is that you want the best sales force structure. So change the Decision Statement to "Determine the best way(s) to structure our sales force." Any time you find you have ruled out the existing alternative by assuming that it is of no use and that something else has to be better, you need to reexamine your Decision Statement.

Develop Mode

In the develop mode, you are out to create a brand new alternative, something that hasn't existed before; you're out to synthesize. By definition, this alternative should optimally conform to the objectives that have been defined; *they* are its design criteria.

The best approach is to look at your 10-weighted objectives and start to design an alternative that best meets them. Then move down to any 9-weighted objectives and, using the criteria they represent, further add to the design. Continue this process through all the successively lower-weighted objectives. As you proceed down the line and expand and refine the design to satisfy the lower-weighted objectives, you'll often come to a point of conflict. The new details being added to satisfy a lower-weighted objective might conflict with an element of the design already prescribed by a higher-weighted objective. What do you do? First, look for other ways to accomplish the lower-weighted criteria. If this doesn't work, go back and examine the specific design elements used to satisfy the higher-weighted objective and see if they can be altered to meet both objectives. If this isn't possible, then weight rules; most likely you will have to abandon satisfying the lower-weighted objective.

There is also another way of handling such a conflict; you can decide to abandon the attempt to create *the* best alternative and proceed to define two—and perhaps later three or four—alternatives, which you can then analyze in the determine mode.

The Meeting

To generate alternatives, the southwest regional office team pored over a map and airline schedules and selected the following list of candidate cities:

A.	Albuquerque	H.	Oklahoma City
B.	Dallas	I.	Phoenix
C.	Denver	J.	Salt Lake City
D.	Fort Worth	K.	San Antonio
E.	Houston	L.	San Diego
F.	Las Vegas	M.	Tucson
G.	Los Angeles		

Step Five: Compare and Choose

At this point, it's all downhill. The bulk of the grunt work has been accomplished. The creative work of establishing and valuing objectives and of generating alternatives is done. Now the Decision Analysis moves into the home stretch as you compare the alternatives to the objectives to determine the best. To do this, you must set up a matrix that arrays the objectives and the alternatives in a manner in which they can be compared. We'll use the southwest regional headquarters matrix that the team developed as an example in this section (Figure 5.2).

Satisfaction Scales

Taking advantage of the relative and comparative powers of numbers, you can use weighting in the Decision Analysis process to express the relative importance of the objectives. Numbers can be employed in a similar fashion to express the degree to which each alternative satisfies each objective.

To determine the degree to which an alternative satisfies an objective, you first need to create a satisfaction scale for the objective. Consider what is being sought—what is being evaluated—by an objective. Now look at the alternatives and reflect how well each accomplishes this end. Select the one—or ones because there may be several that are equal—that provide this best level of satisfaction. Then write a brief description of this level of satisfaction; this defines the top of the satisfaction scale, the 10.

Now, forget about the alternatives for a moment and just think about what would constitute complete failure to satisfy the objective in any way. Write a brief description of this level of satisfaction; it becomes the 0 (zero) at the bottom of your scale. Thus, for the first objective in the example (city size), the team might develop the following satisfaction scale:

Objective: Moderate size area (population)	
Satisfaction Scale	*Score*
Metropolitan Statistical Area size ≤ 500,000	10
Metropolitan Statistical Area size ≥ 2,000,000	0

They would then look at the difference between the two ends of the scale and define one or more interim levels of satisfaction. They might choose to simply define a midpoint and give it a relative fit of 5 on the scale; they might decide to define levels that are equal thirds along the scale, thus defining relative fits of 7 and 3; or they might find some other approach.

DECISION STATEMENT: Select the best location for our southwest regional office

OBJECTIVES	WT	ALTERNATIVES																									
		A		B		C		D		E		F		G		H		I		J		K		L		M	
		SC	WT SC	SC	WT SC	SC	WT SC	SC	WT SC	SC	WT SC	SC	WT SC	SC	WT SC	SC	WT SC	SC	WT SC	SC	WT SC	SC	WT SC	SC	WT SC	SC	WT SC
Moderate size	10																										
Moderate cost of living	10																										
Adequate infrastructure	10																										
Air transportation	9																										
Physical quality	8																										
Aesthetic quality	8																										
Stable economy	7																										
Office workers	7																										
Office space	5																										
Broad economy	5																										
TOTAL WEIGHTED SCORE		▓	▓		▓		▓		▓		▓		▓		▓		▓		▓		▓		▓		▓	

Figure 5.2 Decision Analysis Matrix No. 1

Objective: Moderate size area (population)

Satisfaction Scale		Score
Metropolitan Statistical Area size $\leq$	500,000	10
Metropolitan Statistical Area size $=$	1,000,000	7
Metropolitan Statistical Area size $=$	1,500,000	3
Metropolitan Statistical Area size $\geq$	2,000,000	0

It's important that the defined top of the scale is attainable by at least one alternative—otherwise you'll end up distorting the relativity of the objectives. To illustrate this distortion, suppose you're evaluating the alternatives against a 10-weighted objective; the best alternative(s) would receive a relative fit of 10. Multiplying the weight times the relative fit results in a weighted score—which we will discuss shortly—of 100. However, if the best alternative only has a relative fit of 7, its weighted score would be 70. Thus the effect of the top of the satisfaction scale not being attainable is to effectively reduce the weight of the objective to 7.

Recognize that when you go to use a scale like this, every number, every relative fit (10, 9, 8, 7, 6, 5, 4, 3, 2, 1, 0), is available to you. With some easily quantified objectives, you might choose to define every one of the eleven levels of satisfaction. However, in most cases this isn't necessary or practical. Do what works for you.

Using this scale, the team would enter a score for each alternative, based on where its population placed it, in the appropriate box in the matrix (Figure 5.3).

When evaluating an alternative and placing its score in a matrix, if there is a particular piece of information that is behind an alternative's score, you may wish to also write it in the box so it isn't forgotten. The matrix used in a decision-making meeting is often constructed on several flip charts that provide ample space for such notes. Proceed through this same process for every objective.

Returning to the example, the team might base the satisfaction scale for the second objective on the Consumer Price Index. The third objective might be calculated on typical commuting times. The fourth objective's scale—to illustrate a more subjective approach—might look like this:

Objective: Excellent air transportation access

Satisfaction Scale	Score
Frequent direct flights to most major cities by two or more carriers.	10
Only one direct carrier; others require one connection.	5
No direct carriers; all require connections.	0

DECISION STATEMENT: Select the best location for our southwest regional office

OBJECTIVES	WT	A SC	A WT	B SC	B WT	C SC	C WT	D SC	D WT	E SC	E WT	F SC	F WT	G SC	G WT	H SC	H WT	I SC	I WT	J SC	J WT	K SC	K WT	L SC	L WT	M SC	M WT
Moderate size	10	10		0		2		4		0		9		0		7		1		7		5		0		9	
Moderate cost of living	10																										
Adequate infrastructure	10																										
Air transportation	9																										
Physical quality	8																										
Aesthetic quality	8																										
Stable economy	7																										
Office workers	7																										
Office space	5																										
Broad economy	5																										
TOTAL WEIGHTED SCORE																											

Figure 5.3   Decision Analysis Matrix No. 2

Returning to the first objective, "Moderate size area," the team members could have entered the population of each area into its respective box in the matrix; for the "Moderate cost of living" objective, they could have entered the Consumer Price Indices. They could have entered verbal descriptions in response to "Has adequate infrastructure" and "Excellent air transportation access." But if they had done this, what would they have? They would have the old story of apples and oranges. In short, they would possess a mass of individual pieces of information that offered no easy means of comparison or determining relative gratification. This is avoided when you quantify each input up front in its respective satisfaction scale. By converting every degree of satisfaction to a relative number, all judgments are reduced to a common denominator, to the same form of measurement.

In some cases, a 0 score in a satisfaction scale may be seen as an unacceptable degree of satisfaction. In other words, the bottom of the scale may have been defined as a must or a knockout factor, thus any alternative scoring a 0 is considered a no-go. As we discussed earlier, make sure that a must really and absolutely constitutes a critical death knell before using it as such.

If, in the course of the Compare and Choose step, an alternative appears to be killed either because of a knockout 0 against a weighted objective or because of going over the no-go line on a must objective, put a big red M (must) in the appropriate box but *do not* stop evaluating it. Carry the alternative through the rest of the analysis. Why? We'll cover this shortly.

After the team has continued through the process, setting up a satisfaction scale for each objective and evaluating each alternative against it, it will have a matrix like that shown in Figure 5.4.

So far, the team has used the relative and comparative powers of numbers to reduce apples and oranges to common denominators and reflect two different relativities:

1. The relative importance of the objectives, as expressed by their weights.
2. The degree to which alternatives satisfy objectives, as expressed by their scores.

Now the team members can put the comparative powers of numbers to one more use: They can multiply each alternative's score times the weight of the objective to give a weighted score. The result is shown in Figure 5.5.

Finally, if they add up the weighted scores for each alternative, they get its total weighted score, which offers a comparative picture of how it measures up against the other alternatives (Figure 5.6). In this case, J (Salt Lake City) comes out on top, with A (Albuquerque) for all practical purposes its equal.

DECISION STATEMENT: Select the best location for our southwest regional office

OBJECTIVES	WT	A SC	A WT SC	B SC	B WT SC	C SC	C WT SC	D SC	D WT SC	E SC	E WT SC	F SC	F WT SC	G SC	G WT SC	H SC	H WT SC	I SC	I WT SC	J SC	J WT SC	K SC	K WT SC	L SC	L WT SC	M SC	M WT SC
Moderate size	10	10		0		2		4		0		9		0		7		1		7		5		0		9	
Moderate cost of living	10	8		7		4		7		8		10		10		9		8		9		10		0		10	
Adequate infrastructure	10	10		3		4		7		5		8		0		8		6		9		10		4		8	
Air transportation	9	2		10		10		10		9		7		10		4		9		8		3		8		5	
Physical quality	8	10		8		7		8		7		7		3		8		7		10		9		8		8	
Aesthetic quality	8	8		7		4		6		5		1		10		3		8		7		6		9		7	
Stable economy	7	10		7		4		7		2		7		10		2		6		10		7		9		8	
Office workers	7	9		5		7		6		8		3		2		9		7		10		7		4		6	
Office space	5	8		9		10		7		10		4		7		10		8		9		8		5		8	
Broad economy	5	6		8		5		8		6		0		10		2		7		7		7		9		6	
TOTAL WEIGHTED SCORE																											

Figure 5.4   Decision Analysis Matrix No. 3

OBJECTIVES	WT	A SC	A WT SC	B SC	B WT SC	C SC	C WT SC	D SC	D WT SC	E SC	E WT SC	F SC	F WT SC	G SC	G WT SC	H SC	H WT SC	I SC	I WT SC	J SC	J WT SC	K SC	K WT SC	L SC	L WT SC	M SC	M WT SC
Moderate size	10	10	100	0	0	2	20	4	40	0	0	9	90	0	0	7	70	1	10	7	70	5	50	0	0	9	90
Moderate cost of living	10	8	80	7	70	4	40	7	70	8	80	10	100	10	100	9	90	8	80	9	90	10	100	0	0	10	100
Adequate infrastructure	10	10	100	3	30	4	40	7	70	5	50	8	80	0	0	8	80	6	60	9	90	10	100	4	40	8	80
Air transportation	9	2	18	10	90	10	90	10	90	9	81	7	63	10	90	4	36	9	81	8	72	3	27	8	72	5	45
Physical quality	8	10	80	8	64	7	56	8	64	7	56	7	56	3	24	8	64	7	56	10	80	9	72	8	64	8	64
Aesthetic quality	8	8	64	7	56	4	32	6	48	5	40	1	8	10	80	3	24	8	64	7	56	6	48	8	64	7	56
Stable economy	7	10	70	7	49	4	36	7	49	2	14	7	49	10	70	2	14	6	42	10	70	7	49	9	63	8	56
Office workers	7	9	63	5	35	7	49	6	42	8	56	3	21	2	14	9	63	7	49	10	70	7	49	4	28	6	42
Office space	5	8	40	9	45	10	50	7	35	10	50	4	20	7	35	10	50	8	40	9	45	8	40	5	25	8	40
Broad economy	5	6	30	8	40	5	25	8	40	6	30	0	0	10	50	2	10	7	35	7	35	7	35	9	45	6	30
TOTAL WEIGHTED SCORE																											

Figure 5.5 Decision Analysis Matrix No. 4

DECISION STATEMENT: Select the best location for our southwest regional office

ALTERNATIVES

OBJECTIVES	WT	A SC	A WT SC	B SC	B WT SC	C SC	C WT SC	D SC	D WT SC	E SC	E WT SC	F SC	F WT SC	G SC	G WT SC	H SC	H WT SC	I SC	I WT SC	J SC	J WT SC	K SC	K WT SC	L SC	L WT SC	M SC	M WT SC
Moderate size	10	10	100	0	0	2	20	4	40	0	0	9	90	0	0	7	70	1	10	7	70	5	50	0	0	9	90
Moderate cost of living	10	8	80	7	70	4	40	7	70	8	80	10	100	10	100	9	90	8	80	9	90	10	100	0	0	10	100
Adequate infrastructure	10	10	100	3	30	4	40	7	70	5	50	8	80	0	0	8	80	6	60	9	90	10	100	4	40	8	80
Air transportation	9	2	18	10	90	10	90	10	90	9	81	7	63	10	90	4	36	9	81	8	72	3	27	8	72	5	45
Physical quality	8	10	80	8	64	7	56	8	64	7	56	7	56	3	24	8	64	7	56	10	80	9	72	8	64	8	64
Aesthetic quality	8	8	64	7	56	4	32	6	48	5	40	1	8	10	80	3	24	8	64	7	56	6	48	9	72	7	56
Stable economy	7	10	70	7	49	4	36	7	49	2	14	7	49	10	70	2	14	6	42	10	70	7	49	9	63	8	56
Office workers	7	9	63	5	35	7	49	6	42	8	56	3	21	2	14	9	63	7	49	10	70	7	49	4	28	6	42
Office space	5	8	40	9	45	10	50	7	35	10	50	4	20	7	35	10	50	8	40	9	45	8	40	5	25	8	40
Broad economy	5	6	30	8	40	5	25	8	40	6	30	0	0	10	50	2	10	7	35	7	35	7	35	9	45	6	30
TOTAL WEIGHTED SCORE			645		479		430		548		457		487		463		469		517		678		570		399		603

Figure 5.6 Decision Analysis Matrix No. 5

Considering the objectives that were established, the importance attached to each, and the relative degrees to which they were satisfied, alternatives J and A best fulfill the conditions that were defined.

The significance of these total weighted scores lies solely in their relativity to each other. They *compare* the alternatives. However, by applying weights from 10 to 1 and satisfaction scales from 10 to 0, decision makers operate at a 10% discrimination level. Thus there is room to question whether there is a significant difference in the satisfaction offered by an alternative whose total weighted score is within 10% of the top alternative's score.

One other relativity that decision makers should recognize is how close the best alternative(s) comes to the ideal. To define the ideal, first add up the weights of all the objectives. In this example, the weights column totals 79. Thus, if one alternative had been given a 10 in every satisfaction scale, it would have a total weighted score of 790. That highest possible score defines the ideal. In this example, alternative J with a total score of 678 is at the 86th percentile (678/790 = 86%) relative to the ideal.

Regarding the "Not require more than $200,000 project cost" objective that was put aside earlier by the team, now is an appropriate time to discuss the issue. Why should you continue evaluating an alternative even though it may have struck out against a must or received a knockout 0? Suppose the alternative struck out because its cost was $200,298 when the decision makers had been told that $200,000 was the limit. And just suppose that this alternative's total score was 753, with the next closest being 602. In such a situation, it would be prudent for the decision makers to go to the people holding the purse strings and tell them: "We thought you should be aware that, for an additional $298, you can get a 25% better satisfaction of all the other objectives. What do you want to do?"

There are those who advocate one further step in the Decision Analysis process—that of examining your (tentative) choice for possible adverse consequences. Early in my years of consulting work using Decision Analysis, I found that this is an unnecessary, and dangerous, thing to do. The reason the pursuit of possible adverse consequences can be dangerous is that in the vast majority of real-life situations, it becomes a happy hunting ground for those who are out to support their pet alternative and torpedo all others. Thus it's possible to inject a good bit of bias at the conclusion of an otherwise objective process.

But more important, a factor that can legitimately be identified as a possible adverse consequence is nothing other than a condition, a desired result, that was overlooked when the objectives were originally established. What this says is that, if you leave no stone unturned when you're in the Establish Objectives step, you should have effectively covered all the bases.

Another thing this says is that—at any stage of the Decision Analysis process—if you realize that you've overlooked a relevant objective, don't hesitate to add it.

Second Evaluation

Going through two—or more—evaluations, rounds of creating alternatives and analyzing them, is common in the determine mode of Decision Analysis. In many decision situations, there are an infinite number of alternatives possible. To keep things workable, decision makers will often start out by defining broad, generic, macro-level alternatives for a first cut (first evaluation) comparison against the objectives. They will then take the winner—or perhaps two or three winners if it's a close race—of this first evaluation and manipulate and rearrange their characteristics to create new, more finely tuned, more micro alternatives. The decision makers then take a second trip through Compare and Choose with this second evaluation alternative. That's what the concept of second evaluation is all about.

Also in the determine mode, don't overlook the previously discussed fact that the alternatives may not be mutually exclusive; the best way of achieving the objectives may be to decide to go with a composite of two or more of the alternatives. Combinations of alternatives can be cranked through Compare and Choose as a second evaluation.

A Second Evaluation Example

This example comes from a situation faced by a residential home builder that undertakes extremely large projects across the country. The company was at a point at which several major projects were nearing completion and several new ones were in the wings awaiting start-up. It was an appropriate time for them to look to the future and consider whether their present organizational structure would best serve tomorrow's needs.

Although the ultimate objective of the example is to illustrate the concept of a second evaluation, we can review the concepts of Decision Analysis by briefly examining each step leading up to the second evaluation. For starters, here are the givens that framed the builder's Decision Analysis.

Givens

- Things don't always go as smoothly as we'd like the way we're presently organized.

- Our industry will be facing increasing governmental regulation in the future.
- There will be fewer mega-project opportunities in the future.
- Speedier decision making is going to be the order of the day in the future.
- Future projects will require greater attention to the project's shopping and cultural amenities.

Decision Statement

Determine our optimum future organization structure.

Objectives and Values

Here is an abridged list of the objectives that were used, accompanied by their assigned weights:

10 Maximum ability to expand and contract to manage varying project loads.
10 Provide an adequate level of checks, balances, and controls.
 9 Provide for appropriate speed and quality of decision making.
 8 Maximize the utilization of our unique "product" capabilities.
 8 Maximum ability to attract and retain quality people.
 7 Minimum confusion over who's responsible for what.
 7 Provide adequate growth and development opportunities for our people.
 6 Minimum potential to get too inbred.
 6 Maximum flexibility to use people wherever they're needed.
 5 Lean and mean.

Alternatives

A. *Present structure as is, no change:* functional executives (financial, marketing, planning, etc.) and senior project directors (largest projects) report to the president. Other project directors report to functional executives.

B. *Project-oriented structure:* project directors report to the president. Each project director has his or her own functional organization (financial, marketing, planning).

C. *Functional structure:* functional executives (financial, marketing, planning) report to the president. Each project's functional managers report to their respective functional executives.

D. *Matrix structure:* functional executives (financial, marketing, planning) and project directors all report to the president. Each project's functional managers report to both their respective functional executives and to their project director.

E. *Geographic structure:* regional vice presidents report to the president. Functional executives (financial, marketing, planning) report to the president. Project directors report to their respective regional vice presidents.

Satisfaction Scales

The following are representative samplings of the scales that were used:

Objective: Maximum ability to expand and contract to manage varying project loads

Satisfaction Scale	Score
Can roll with the punches quickly and easily	10
Some constraints that could be handled over time	5
Very rigid and inflexible	0

Objective: Maximize the utilization of our unique "product" capabilities

Satisfaction Scale	Score
Excellent ability to emphasize target product areas	10
Some minor, livable shortcomings	5
Major, undesirable shortcomings	0

Objective: Maximum flexibility to use people wherever they're needed

Satisfaction Scale	Score
Roving specialty teams, have guns will travel	10
Some red tape to make it happen	5
Cast in concrete	0

Compare and Choose

Looking at Figure 5.7, you can see that D (the matrix organization structure) came out on top by a significant margin. However, that doesn't say that it can't be improved. To attempt to improve D, the first thing the builder's team did was to go down the column that shows D's scores against each objective. Any place where D didn't get a high score, the team looked for an alternative that did and considered why it scored higher. The team members asked if there was anything they could learn from the higher-scored alternative relative to a way to modify D and improve its satisfaction of this objective.

DECISION STATEMENT: Determine our optimum future organization structure														
		ALTERNATIVES												
		A		B		C		D		E		F		G
OBJECTIVES	WT	SC	WT SC	SC	WT SC	SC	WT SC	SC	WT SC	SC	WT SC	SC	WT SC	SC	WT SC
Expand and contract	10	4	40	0	0	10	100	9	90	3	30				
Checks and balances	10	6	60	3	30	5	50	10	100	7	70				
Decision making	9	6	54	10	90	2	18	5	45	4	36				
Utilize capabilities	8	3	24	0	0	8	64	10	80	3	24				
Attract/retain people	8	5	40	10	80	8	64	7	56	4	32				
Minimum confusion	7	6	42	10	70	0	0	6	42	7	49				
People development	7	5	35	10	70	8	56	7	49	4	28				
Not get inbred	6	7	42	4	24	5	30	10	60	5	30				
People flexibility	6	5	30	2	12	6	36	10	60	4	24				
Lean and mean	5	10	50	0	0	2	10	5	25	7	35				
TOTAL WEIGHTED SCORE			417		376		428		607		358				

Figure 5.7 Decision Analysis Matrix No. 6

As far as satisfying "Provide for appropriate speed and quality of decision making" was concerned, the team felt that the reason for B's high relative fit of 10 was obvious and that B (project-oriented structure) and D were at opposite poles on this one; to change D to approach B would destroy D's matrix concept. As far as D's less than optimum showing, a relative fit of 7, against "Maximum ability to attract and retain quality people" was concerned, the team members came to the same conclusion as they had with D's poor satisfaction of "Minimum confusion over who's responsible for what." Likewise D was examined against the high scorers in the "People development" and "Lean and mean" objectives with the same conclusion.

Considering that Alternative C (functional structure)—with a significantly lower score than D—was slightly ahead of A, their present structure, they decided to see if C could be improved. As far as "Provide an adequate level of checks, balances, and controls" was concerned, looking at D, E (geographic structure), and A (present structure), they came up with the

DECISION STATEMENT: Determine our optimum future organization structure															
		ALTERNATIVES													
		A		B		C		D		E		F		G	
OBJECTIVES	WT	SC	WT SC	SC	WT SC	SC	WT SC	SC	WT SC	SC	WT SC	SC	WT SC	SC	WT SC
Expand and contract	10	4	40	0	0	10	100	9	90	3	30	10	100		
Checks and balances	10	6	60	3	30	5	50	10	100	7	70	6	60		
Decision making	9	6	54	10	90	2	18	5	45	4	36	7	63		
Utilize capabilities	8	3	24	0	0	8	64	10	80	3	24	8	64		
Attract/retain people	8	5	40	10	80	8	64	7	56	4	32	8	64		
Minimum confusion	7	6	42	10	70	0	0	6	42	7	49	9	63		
People development	7	5	35	10	70	8	56	7	49	4	28	9	63		
Not get inbred	6	7	42	4	24	5	30	10	60	5	30	6	36		
People flexibility	6	5	30	2	12	6	36	10	60	4	24	11	66		
Lean and mean	5	10	50	0	0	2	10	5	25	7	35	9	45		
TOTAL WEIGHTED SCORE			417		376		428		607		358		624		

Figure 5.8   Decision Analysis Matrix No. 7

idea of creating an executive vice president level that would oversee all new projects—that is, projects that were less than 50% completed. This led to the creation of a new alternative, F, which was defined as:

F. *Functional/new project structure:* Same as Alternative C (functional structure) except that project directors of projects not half completed will report to an executive vice president.

They quickly realized that F would also offer significant improvement in satisfying the "Decision making" objective since the new projects were the ones in which the need was the greatest and they would all be under the same umbrella. The same held true for the "Minimum confusion" objective. As far as "People flexibility" was concerned, the team felt that F would even be better than D because, again, new projects really need this flexibility.

This new alternative was added to the matrix (Figure 5.8).

One more significant point needs to be made about the second evaluation concept. Earlier, I emphasized that every satisfaction scale should be constructed so that at least one alternative can achieve a score of 10—otherwise the relative weights of the objectives would be distorted. In a second evaluation Decision Analysis, it's possible to come up with a new alternative that satisfies an objective even better than is defined by the 10 at the top of its satisfaction scale. If this is valid, then obviously it should be factored into the analysis. One way of doing this is to go back and reconstruct the scale and then change all the relevant numbers in the Compare and Choose matrix. A much easier approach is to simply mentally expand the scale upward to include 11, 12, and so on—to whatever number is required to reflect the higher satisfaction.

As you can see in Figure 5.8, that is what the builder's team did regarding alternative F and its satisfaction of the "People flexibility" objective. At this stage, the reference base is strong enough to prevent one or two scores higher than 10 from wreaking havoc with the relativity of the weights.

In the end, although the numerical difference between D and F was insignificant, the builder's team felt that Alternative F would be an easier transition and chose to go with it.

Thumbs Down?

On rare occasions, decision makers will complete their analysis, look at the alternative that came out on top, and conclude that they "don't like it." For all practical purposes, there are two likely explanations for this:

1. A pet alternative didn't come out on top and the decision makers' egos, biases, emotions, or whatever have taken command.
2. One or more important objectives were never thought of in the Establish Objectives step.

Yes, there also could be flaws in the weights assigned to the objectives, or in the satisfaction scales, but these are much less likely. When this rare happening does occur, the decision makers should pause and reflect on *why* they don't like the top alternative. They should get out their Objective Setting Checklist and pore over it to see what objectives, if any, they overlooked. If any are found, they can plug them into the analysis and redo it. But beware: This setting is ripe for—consciously or subconsciously—stacking the deck.

If no missing objectives are uncovered, and if no flaws are found in the weighting or satisfaction scales, then perhaps it's time to own up to that thing called bias.

The World of Decision Analysis

You've just gone through in-depth illustrations of the application of Decision Analysis tools to decisions involving selecting a location and an organization structure. But there's a wide world of other types of Planned Future Change situations out there in which this thinking process can be used. For example:

- Determine how to stifle a cash flow problem that is threatening a division's life.
- Determine how to standardize widely varying accounting procedures in an organization's worldwide operations.
- Develop the optimum specifications for a new machine that will extend the product line's range into uncharted waters.
- Decide which government agency should administer a new program.
- Develop an order of attack to resolve a myriad of problems in a new acquisition.
- Decide how to restructure manufacturing operations to eliminate excess capacity brought about by the implementation of a new technology.
- Choose which competitors' products to license in order to expand a product line.
- Decide the best type of sales organization to use in overseas markets.

In Summary: Decision Analysis

The major concept steps of Decision Analysis are:

1. Define the Decision Statement

    - Purpose
        Select/Determine/Develop
        Best/Optimum
        KISS
        True Choice/Net Effect (not yes/no)
    - Level
        Preceding: known or assumption?

2. Establish Objectives
    - Results or outputs

   • Resources or inputs
   • Checklist
   • Single variable

3. Value Objectives
   • Weight 10 to 1—relative importance
   • Must = absolute cutoff

4. Generate Alternatives
   • Select: off-the-shelf
   • Determine: representative cross section
     Possibly two (or more) evaluations
   • Develop: create/design

5. Compare and Choose
   • Satisfaction Scales
     Score 10 to 0
     Knockout 0/Must
   • Weights x Scores
   • Total Weighted Scores
     Second evaluation?
     Is the must real?
     Relativity

6

Implementation Planning

The Implementation Planning process is *not* one of the three basic thinking processes. It is an application of the develop mode of Decision Analysis coupled with the creation of appropriate worksheets to define and track the details.

The chapter on Decision Analysis focused on the fundamental thinking process for optimizing a choice. However, most complex decisions are not made to happen simply by saying "Let's go do it." Most complex decisions require many events to happen in an appropriate sequence if the choice is to become a reality. Thus an Implementation Plan is called for, and there's a seven-step process for developing it:

1. Formulate the Plan Statement
2. Identify Plan Objectives
3. Identify Plan Components
4. Schedule Events and Times
5. Revisit Components—Additional Analyses
6. Perform Objectives Test
7. Redraft the Plan

Because of the number of steps in Implementation Planning, and because they're relatively straightforward, we'll move right into the meeting and illustrate the concepts with that example.

One point before we start. There are many project-management software packages on the market that do an excellent job of structuring the elements of an Implementation Plan. However, for many small, not sophisticated plans, it's a lot quicker and simpler to do them by hand unless you're already an expert with such software. Also, roughing out the elements of a plan via the process we're about to discuss often simplifies transferring the plan to the software.

Step One: Formulate the Plan Statement

Just because everyone is comfortable with a particular conclusion does not make that conclusion a reality; it doesn't make it happen. The problem-solving team has decided to locate the southwest regional office in Salt Lake City, but a lot of things have to be made to happen before the organization's people are happily settled in there doing what they're supposed to do to effectively handle the southwest region business.

First, just as the Decision Statement was the focal point for the Decision Analysis process, a Plan Statement is the focal point around which you develop an Implementation Plan. A Plan Statement is analogous to a develop mode Decision Statement—after all, when you create a plan what are you out to do but to create an alternative? In the example we've been using, the team formulated this Plan Statement:

> Develop the best plan for getting our Salt Lake City regional office operational.

As you can see, everything that has been said about a Decision Statement carries over into a Plan Statement. And as we move on to the next step, the parallel continues.

Step Two: Identify Plan Objectives

A certain set of objectives was deemed necessary to shape and direct a Decision Analysis, and the same is true for an Implementation Plan. Although these implementation objectives are developed in the same manner, they generally are fewer in number and are defined in a more macro or all-encompassing fashion than in a Decision Analysis. The management of the company setting up the regional office had already decreed one Plan Objective:

> We can't spend more than $200,000 on setting up the regional office.

The team identified other Plan Objectives, including these two:

1. Must be fully operational by next July.
2. Must be at least 50% staffed by present personnel.

Notice how that "must" word—the same term whose use was discouraged back in the chapter on Decision Analysis—crept so easily into the scene here. And again, the same discouragement is offered: The team members should ask if they really believe the whole concept would die if it didn't get off the ground until the first week in August. Do they really think it would be ineffective if they had to staff it with 60% of the people being new hires from the Salt Lake City area? Most likely, the answer would be "No" on both counts.

Too often in planning situations, once the macro course has been decided, people adopt a full-speed-ahead, we-don't-need-to-do-any-more-thinking outlook. Suddenly everything has to be done yesterday. "Must" objectives often encourage this. Realistically, such musts are usually questionable, perhaps even dangerous. Practically, they can be useful from the standpoint of making the target more definitive, of spotlighting a more rigid benchmark.

So, the message here is that while such definitive objectives can be useful up front as guides in the development of the plan, be judicious about accepting them at face value when it comes time to measure the plan against them.

One closing point on Plan Objectives: Because their role is to serve as overall macro guidelines for the development of the plan, usually there isn't any need to determine their relative importance or value them.

Step Three: Identify Plan Components

Now the team was ready to assemble a list of the major decisions that have to be made, tasks to be undertaken, actions that must happen, things to be accomplished, for the overall plan to happen. Reflecting on the earlier discussions about the southwest regional office, the team saw that several of these components had already been identified:

• Select the best part of the city . . .
• Select the best site/building . . .
• What functions should be handled in a regional office?
• Who should we move there to staff it?

Working with the decision makers to expand this list yielded additional components, including these:

- Get letterhead and forms printed.
- Move our people to Salt Lake City.
- Hire the additional local people we need.
- Train the new hires.
- Set up telephone and computer lines.
- Notify our southwest regional customers.
- Determine our equipment needs.
- Determine how much space we need.

At this point the group started to slow down, so the leader stopped the process of determining components at that time. Although the list was not complete, the leader wasn't worried. In fact, if the list was complete—assuming *complete* lists are possible—it would most likely be too unwieldy to work with.

Note that what the group has just done is nothing other than going back to Situation Assessment's Recognize step. It's not impossible that some of the issues the group members identified will subsequently need to be subjected to the Separate step; some might even require their own Decision Analyses.

Step Four: Schedule Events and Times

A plan is nothing other than a road map that spells out what is supposed to happen and when. The problem solvers have identified what has to happen; now they have to create a time frame for their accomplishment. A time frame can be influenced by several factors such as:

- An absolute deadline date by which the plan must be operational if it is going to succeed.
- Particular time windows for particular happenings ("We will not move our people while school is in session").
- Independent/dependent relationships among the components.

Back in the Decision Analysis chapter, the decision makers identified the independent decision as:

D1 = Determine the best location for our southwest regional office.

They also recognized, at that time, three sequential dependent decisions:

D2 = Should we place it downtown or . . . ?

D3 = What functions should . . . ?

D4 = Who should staff it?

However, they now have a greatly expanded list of Plan Components, some of which *may* have dependent relationships to the above and/or to each other. To begin to work with these components, they must first be collected in a list and each given an identifying label (the team used letters for this). The result is shown in Figure 6.1. Note that there hasn't been any attempt to determine interrelationships—that comes next. What you see is simply a worksheet that is a gathering place for the components identified thus far.

Looking at the items in the list, the team proceeded to identify interrelationships between them. They noted in the Depends On column which other components, if any, that each component was linked to or dependent on (Figure 6.2).

The next step the team took is the heart of the planning process. It involves establishing a time frame for the accomplishment of each component; it factors in time elements such as deadline dates and time windows. The net effect is that an overall priority order of attack is developed.

To begin with, the problem solvers decided the size of the time increments they were going to use in this first cut at the drafting of the plan. They felt that weekly was too tight and monthly was too loose, so they set-

PLAN STATEMENT: Develop the best plan for getting our Salt Lake City regional office operational			
COMPONENTS		DEPENDS ON	WHO?
A	Select the best part of the city for our office		
B	Select the best site/building for our office		
C	Determine what functions to perform on a regional basis		
D	Select the best people to move there and staff it		
E	Get letterhead and forms printed		
F	Move our people to Salt Lake City		
G	Hire the additional local people we need		
H	Train the new hires		
I	Set up telephone and computer lines		
J	Notify our southwest regional customers		
K	Determine our equipment needs		
L	Determine how much space we need		

Figure 6.1   Plan Components Worksheet No. 1

PLAN STATEMENT: Develop the best plan for getting our Salt Lake City regional office operational			
COMPONENTS		**DEPENDS ON**	**WHO?**
A	Select the best part of the city for our office		
B	Select the best site/building for our office	A, L	
C	Determine what functions to perform on a regional basis		
D	Select the best people to move there and staff it	C	
E	Get letterhead and forms printed	B, I	
F	Move our people to Salt Lake City	D	
G	Hire the additional local people we need	C, D	
H	Train the new hires	G	
I	Set up telephone and computer lines	B, C	
J	Notify our southwest regional customers	B, I	
K	Determine our equipment needs	C	
L	Determine how much space we need	C, K	

Figure 6.2   Plan Components Worksheet No. 2

tled on semimonthly, to be designated by Roman numerals I and II. They then entered each component into an Events and Times Worksheet (Figure 6.3). For purposes of this illustration, we'll assume that the team was working at the end of September. Considering that they faced a deadline of next July, the decision makers realized that failure to meet target dates in the early stages of the plan's implementation—or other unforeseen circumstances—could cause them to have to resort to weekly increments in subsequent iterations of the plan. However, they saw that as a bridge to be crossed if and when they got to it.

The time increments used in an Events and Times Worksheet can be absolute—that is, defined by actual calendar dates—or they can be relative—that is, defined by elapsed time. A company that's in the business of manufacturing and installing large, standardized machinery, for example, might develop generic elapsed-time Events and Times charts using time increments such as week 1, week 2, and so on. However, the Salt Lake City team obviously had to use absolute timing. These decision makers decided to:

- Start A (Select the best part of the city....) immediately and expect it to be finished in two weeks.
- Start C (Determine what functions to perform....) immediately, figuring it can be done in two weeks as well.
- Once the answer to C is known, start K (Determine our equipment needs), which could require a month.
- As soon as K is known, work on L (Determine how much space we need), which could be done in two weeks.

Their chart, as it stood at that point, is shown in Figure 6.3.

Someone suggested that they should move on to B (Select the best site ...), but another person said, "No, we should do D (Select the best people ...) before B so that at least some of the people to be moved there can be involved in B." Someone else responded with, "Wait a minute, those people should participate in A as well."

PLAN STATEMENT: Develop the best plan for getting our Salt Lake City regional office operational					
TIME PERIOD	EVENTS—PLANNED		EVENTS—ACTUAL		Why the deviation?
	Start	Finish	Start	Finish	
Oct I	A, C				
Oct II	K	A, C			
Nov I					
Nov II	L	K			
Dec I		L			
Dec II					
Jan I					
Jan II					
Feb I					
Feb II					
Mar I					
Mar II					
Apr I					
Apr II					
May I					
May II					
June I					
June II					
July I					
July II					

Figure 6.3   Events and Times Worksheet No. 1

The problem solvers quickly decided to cross out A from Oct I and Oct II. They then proceeded as follows:

- Start D as soon as C is finished. Because this could require some jockeying around as employees discuss potential relocation with their families, and so on, it was felt this could take up to three months.
- A was moved accordingly, with B to follow immediately with the expectation that it could be accomplished in two weeks. Although there was some discussion whether the people to be moved should be involved in K as well, it was felt that this wasn't necessary.

At this point, their worksheet looked like Figure 6.4.

The decision makers then felt that they had better enter the July deadline date before they got much further along. Considering the "We will not

PLAN STATEMENT: Develop the best plan for getting our Salt Lake City regional office operational					
TIME PERIOD	EVENTS—PLANNED		EVENTS—ACTUAL		Why the deviation?
	Start	Finish	Start	Finish	
Oct I	C				
Oct II	K, D	C			
Nov I					
Nov II	L	K			
Dec I		L			
Dec II					
Jan I					
Jan II	A	D			
Feb I	B	A			
Feb II		B			
Mar I					
Mar II					
Apr I					
Apr II					
May I					
May II					
June I					
June II					
July I					
July II					

Figure 6.4   Events and Times Worksheet No. 2

move our people while school is in session" dictum, they decided to consider July II as the deadline. They proceeded as follows:

- F (Move our people) must be completed by July I, therefore start it two weeks earlier.
- H (Train the new hires) must be completed by July I; since we may bring some people to the corporate office for a couple of weeks, we'd better allow a total of a month for this.
- G (Hire the additional local people) could take a month and a half, so we'll need to back it off from H.
- Considering the special, tractor-feed forms we'll need (decided in C) that normally take two months, adding a month's safety factor, we'll back off E (Get letterhead and forms printed) from July I.
- We can't start E until we know the results of I (Set up telephone and computer lines), so we'll back I off from Apr I, allowing a month.
- We should give our customers three-months' advance notice, so we'll start J (Notify our southwest regional customers) in Apr II with a couple of follow-ups.

The problem solvers' completed worksheet resembled Figure 6.5.

So there you have the initial draft of the Events and Times plan for making the southwestern regional office a reality.

Let's pause for a minute and talk about the Actual columns in the Events and Times worksheet. The purpose of any plan is to define and describe an ideal; the reality of any plan is that some events may not happen as planned. Any time an event fails to happen on time, it has the potential to impact the timing—or even the structure—of subsequent events. Thus, as a plan is being worked, the actual happenings should be recorded en route along with explanations of any deviations from the planned happenings. This serves two purposes. The immediate purpose is to trigger any necessary changes in subsequent events due to their linkages to and their dependencies on the missed event. The second purpose is to provide a historical record from which the organization can learn—from its mistakes—how to plan better in the future. We will examine this in more detail later.

One important step remained: the assignment of responsibility for making each of these components happen. *One* person, preferably someone from the original problem-solving team, was made responsible for each component (Figure 6.6). This person could choose to set up his or her own team to help carry out the components, completely delegate the task to someone else, or do whatever else would work best. The important point was that one person would be accountable. Joint responsibility, two or

PLAN STATEMENT: Develop the best plan for getting our Salt Lake City regional office operational					
TIME PERIOD	EVENTS—PLANNED		EVENTS—ACTUAL		Why the deviation?
	Start	Finish	Start	Finish	
Oct I	C				
Oct II	K, D	C			
Nov I					
Nov II	L	K			
Dec I		L			
Dec II					
Jan I					
Jan II	A	D			
Feb I	B	A			
Feb II		B			
Mar I	I				
Mar II					
Apr I	E	I			
Apr II	G, J				
May I					
May II					
June I	H	G			
June II	F				
July I		F, H, E			
July II		J			

Figure 6.5   Events and Times Worksheet No. 3

more people, is almost a guaranteed invitation to trouble and things not happening according to plan.

Step Five: Revisit Components

Once an overall plan had been established, it was appropriate to revisit the components and take a look at what lay ahead.

Additional Analyses

As far as A, B, C, and D were concerned, the problem solvers had long ago recognized them as situations requiring Decision Analyses. Moreover, because Bill had been given the responsibility for accomplishing A and B, the implication was that both of these could be handled by the same team.

E was simply an action to be undertaken at the proper time—there wasn't any concern or uncertainty present there. The problem solvers deter-

PLAN STATEMENT: Develop the best plan for getting our Salt Lake City regional office operational		
COMPONENTS	DEPENDS ON	WHO?
A	Select the best part of the city for our office		Bill
B	Select the best site/building for our office	A, L	Bill
C	Determine what functions to perform on a regional basis		Betty
D	Select the best people to move there and staff it	C	Joe
E	Get letterhead and forms printed	B, I	Betty
F	Move our people to Salt Lake City	D	Ed
G	Hire the additional local people we need	C, D	Karen
H	Train the new hires	G	Jean
I	Set up telephone and computer lines	B, C	Mary
J	Notify our southwest regional customers	B, I	Dick
K	Determine our equipment needs	C	Betty
L	Determine how much space we need	C, K	Harry

Figure 6.6   Plan Components Worksheet No. 3

mined that F would probably require a Decision Analysis along the lines of "Select the best moving company (or companies) to use." It could also require an Implementation Plan of its own: something like "Develop the best plan for moving our people to Salt Lake City." This would be an interesting plan to develop because most likely it would involve timing variables completely outside the company's control, such as those relating to when each employee being moved had to be out of his or her present residence, when employees' new homes would be available to them, when their children would be out of school.

Although G and H had been assigned to different people, clearly there were many decisions to be made within these two components and most likely a separate plan would have to be developed that focused on all the elements of G and H.

I and J appeared to be fairly straightforward actions to be undertaken at the right time. Although K and L required some decision making, most likely these would be simple routine determinations based on the outcome of C.

The plan the team developed evolved from the completion of the first of what was initially recognized as a sequence of four Decision Analyses. The plan established a time frame for the accomplishment of the three remaining analyses. However, the act of constructing the plan also revealed several other Decision Analyses (F, G, and H) that would need to be undertaken along the way. The act of constructing the plan also brought to light other situations of sufficient complexity (F, G, and H) that could each require an Implementation Plan of its own.

After all of a team's plans have been built, a common tendency is to want to combine them all into one overall master plan down to every last nitty-gritty detail. Carrying out this idea might make a systems expert's day, but it often does more harm than good for several reasons. Consider the example. First, the detailed plans for F, G, and H couldn't realistically be constructed for several months. Why force premature, fictitious versions of them—which ultimately will be changed—just for the sake of having one big and possibly cluttered picture? Second, people working in their own specialized areas usually find it infinitely easier to follow a micro plan that contains only the components they need to relate to. If a question comes up about the macro master plan, they can always refer to it.

The important point to recognize is that any component in the initial plan that may be felt to include more than a couple of obvious, simple components within it should be broken down into a sub-plan. Likewise, it's not impossible that the development of a sub-plan might bring to light one or more components for which sub-sub-plans should be developed.

An initial plan should be broken down into as many sub-plans and sub-sub-plans as may be necessary for the problem solvers to get to the point where they feel they have a composite that they can validly test against the plan objectives. Obviously if this leads to a plethora of sub-plans and sub-sub-plans, it may be necessary to pull all these together into an overall master plan before this testing can be done.

Sub-Plans

When the A and B components team—which included a couple of people who would be moving to Salt Lake City—first met, its members felt they definitely needed to construct a sub-plan to use for tracking and managing their responsibilities.

Regarding the statement for Component B, "Select the best site/building for our office," they quickly decided to eliminate the word "site" from it because this implied selecting a piece of ground and constructing their own building. In light of the overall timing for this project, they felt this was not a viable alternative. Thus Component B became "Select the best building for our office."

They then proceeded to develop a list of the components in their sub-plan:

- Visit Salt Lake City to get the lay of the land.
- Select a realtor to assist us.
- Visit the buildings potentially available to us.
- Give the realtor our specs.
- Decide the best part of the city for our office.
- Select the best building.
- Meet with the building's representative.
- Negotiate a lease.
- Determine how long the lease should be.
- Get headquarters' okay on the lease.
- Sign the lease.
- Determine what alterations, if any, are needed.
- Arrange to get the alterations done.
- Verify that the office is ready for us to move in.

They then developed the A and B Team Plan Components Worksheet (Figure 6.7). Note that the group members chose to list the components on the worksheet in the sequence in which they would (most likely) be accomplished as opposed to waiting to do it on the Events and Times Worksheet. Make the process work for you. There's no law that says you must hold off determining the relative timing until you get to the Events and Times stage. If you're comfortable doing it at this earlier point in the process, so be it. You can always modify it, if necessary, at the Events and Times step.

When it was time to move on to an Events and Times Worksheet, the group members paused to think about the time increments they should use. Their conclusion was that this sub-plan should be broken down week by week. It was now the third week in January; the original master plan called for Components A and B to be completed by the end of February. The group members felt this timing was unrealistic—they decided to develop their sub-plan as best they could and if they felt it couldn't be accomplished by then, they'd go back to top management and plead their case.

The sub-plan they developed is shown in the A and B Team Events and Times Worksheet (Figure 6.8).

The sub-plan the group developed, if followed, would require changing the timing of Components I and E on the master plan. They met with Mary (responsible for I) and Betty (responsible for E) and discussed the situation. Mary and Betty both left to make a couple of telephone calls to update their data. When they returned, they both agreed to modify the master

PLAN STATEMENT: Develop the best plan for selecting the building for our Salt Lake City regional office		
COMPONENTS	DEPENDS ON	WHO?
A1	Select a realtor to assist us	A3	Bill
A2	Give the realtor our specs	A1	Bill
A3	Visit Salt Lake City to get the lay of the land		Bill
A4	Decide the best part of the city for our office	A2	Bill
B1	Visit the buildings potentially available to us	A4	Bill
B2	Select the best building	B1	John
B3	Determine how long the lease should be	B5	John
B4	Determine what alterations, if any, are needed	B2	John
B5	Meet with the building's representative	B2	Bill
B6	Negotiate a lease	B3	Bill
B7	Get headquarters' okay on the lease	B6	Bill
B8	Sign the lease	B7	Bill
B9	Arrange to get the alterations done (if needed)	B4, B7	John
B10	Verify that the office is ready for us	B9	John

Figure 6.7   A and B Team Plan Components Worksheet

plan. The result of this second draft (no changes had been made at the earlier reviews) appears in Figure 6.9.

Other Models

Visibility is a key element in Implementation Planning. It's the old story of a picture being worth a thousand words. You have seen several examples of this as you proceeded through this book. There are many ways in which critical resources, such as people's time, machinery or factory limitations, computer capacity, and the like, can be visibly tracked by variations on the plan worksheet and events and times themes. For example, the group working on the A and B sub-plan felt that their timing was going to be so tight that they should create a picture of the demands placed on it. This led to the A and B Team Time Allocation Chart shown in Figure 6.10.

Some organizations might choose to convert the finalized Events and Times charts into a Gantt (time progression) chart. For particularly

TIME PERIOD	EVENTS—PLANNED		EVENTS—ACTUAL		Why the deviation?
	Start	Finish	Start	Finish	

PLAN STATEMENT:
Develop the best plan for getting our Salt Lake City regional office operational

TIME PERIOD	Start	Finish	Start	Finish	Why the deviation?
Jan 4	A1				
Feb 1					
Feb 2	A2	A1, A2			
Feb 3	A3, A4, B1, B2, B3	A3, A4, B1, B2, B3			
Feb 4	B4, B5, B6	B4, B5, B6			
Mar 1	B7, B8	B7, B8			
Mar 2	B9	B9			
Mar 3					
Mar 4					
Apr 1					
Apr 2					
Apr 3					
Apr 4					
May 1					
May 2					
May 3					
May 4	B10	B10			
June 1					
June 2					
June 3					

Figure 6.8   A and B Team Events and Times Worksheet

lengthy and complex plans, they may want to convert them to a PERT (Program Evaluation Review Technique) or CPM (Critical Path Method) chart. Or they may want to crank the data into one of the many software programs designed for creating visual planning documents and tracking them. This gets into territory beyond the fundamental scope of this book, but if you make such a move, be sure you or your computer people know how the software functions and that the need truly exists before doing it. The last thing you'd want would be to develop an excellent plan only to have it get in trouble because of software sickness.

Step Six: Perform Objectives Test

During the second step in developing the Implementation Plan, the regional office team had established a brief list of Plan Objectives:

• Must not cost more than $200,000.
• Must be fully operational by July 31.
• Must be at least 50% staffed by present personnel.

When the first draft of the plan is a fait accompli, it's time to step back and assess how it stacks up against the Plan Objectives. In our example, at the outset it might seem that the first and third objectives might not mesh. This is something that should be brought to top management's attention immediately along with the question "Where's the give? If we can't move 50% of the staff there and start it up for $200,000, do we cut down the number of people we move and increase the local hiring or will you allow us more than $200,000?" Here are a couple of Plan Objectives that are in opposition to each other. Because of their "must" perspective, they have the potential to kill the regional office. Whether this should realistically be permitted to happen needs to be resolved.

TIME PERIOD	EVENTS—PLANNED		EVENTS—ACTUAL		Why the deviation?
	Start	Finish	Start	Finish	
Oct I	C				
Oct II	K, D	C			
Nov I					
Nov II	L	K			
Dec I		L			
Dec II					
Jan I					
Jan II	A	D			
Feb I	B	A			
Feb II		B			
Mar I	I				
Mar II					
Apr I	E	I			
Apr II	G, J, E	I			
May I					
May II					
June I	H	G			
June II	F				
July I		F, H, E			
July II		J			

PLAN STATEMENT:
Develop the best plan for getting our Salt Lake City regional office operational

Figure 6.9   Events and Times Worksheet No. 4

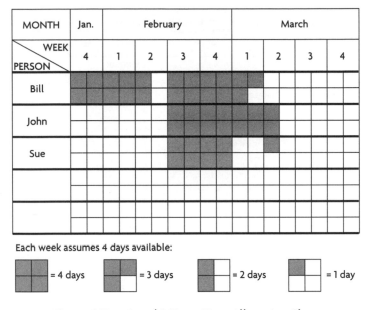

MONTH	Jan.	February					March			
WEEK PERSON	4	1	2	3	4	1	2	3	4
Bill									
John									
Sue									

Each week assumes 4 days available:

■ = 4 days   ◧ = 3 days   ◨ = 2 days   □ = 1 day

Figure 6.10   A and B Team Time Allocation Chart

A delegation of team members discussed these concerns with the company president. His response was that the $200,000 cap was more important than the percentage of local staffing. He also indicated that while the $200,000 was an important target, it wasn't cast in concrete; however, if the team members felt they were going to have difficulty staying within it, they should discuss the situation with him as soon as they became aware of it.

When dealing with an objective that has a finite limit—like "Must not cost more than $200,000"—it can be helpful to construct a Resource Allocation Worksheet to track the consumption of the resource. In this example, team members reviewed the Plan Components Worksheets they had compiled thus far and entered Components F, H, I, K, A3, and B9 into the Objectives Test Worksheet (Figure 6.11). They excluded E (letterheads and forms) because it was considered a normal cost of business regardless of where it was incurred. The individuals responsible for each of these components were asked to develop an initial guesstimate of the "Amount Required" within two weeks.

From the overall plan as it now stood, it appeared that the second Plan Objective could be met.

PLAN STATEMENT: Develop the best plan for getting our Salt Lake City regional office operational			
RESOURCE: Project funding	Total amount available: $200,000		
COMPONENTS	Amount Required	Cumulative	Actual
F Move our people to Salt Lake City			
H Train the new hires			
I Set up telephone and computer lines			
K Determine our equipment needs			
A3 Visit Salt Lake City to get the lay of the land			
B9 Arrange to get the alterations done			

Figure 6.11   Objectives Test Worksheet

Step Seven: Redraft the Plan

A couple of times the plan developed thus far has been referred to as the first draft. Why? Because any plan of any consequence that is cast in concrete the first time around is either so evident that it doesn't deserve to be called a plan or so loose that it's likely be wasting resources. Construction of the plan in this example was started at the end of September; it would be ten months before it was accomplished. In these months, a lot could happen: a key, overlooked component could surface; a major competitor could acquire your largest customer in the region, thus raising doubts about the wisdom of proceeding with the plan; perhaps . . . ? But let's not get ahead of ourselves. These are issues for Potential Problem Analysis, which is the subject of the next chapter.

Any Implementation Plan should be periodically reviewed and, if necessary, revised according to the latest history and expectations. In the case of the southwest regional office plan, the team decided to review and update it formally every other month. Thus this plan could go through four more drafts (at the end of the second, fourth, sixth, and eighth months) before it is filed in the archives as mission accomplished.

Perform Analysis Review

The eighth step that should be undertaken at this point is different in kind from the seven steps involved in developing the plan. This final step involves examining what ultimately actually happened against what was initially planned to happen. Before a plan is filed in the archives, the planning team should meet to examine every deviation between the planned and the actual to see what can be learned from these happenings so errors aren't repeated in future plans. For example, they should go back to the Events and Times Worksheets, examine any differences between the planned and actual happenings, and fill in the "Why the deviation?" column.

Suppose a plan was met perfectly. Is an Analysis Review still appropriate? The answer is "Yes." It's possible that the "perfection" was the result of a plan that was too loose, with too much "give" in it; it's possible that the plan could have been tighter. If so, then you just might learn some valuable lessons for the next time.

The World of Implementation Planning

You've now gone through an in-depth illustration of the application of Implementation Planning to a situation involving the start-up of a new office. But there's a wide world of other types of situations in which this thinking process can be used. For example:

- Implementing a new sales compensation program.
- Setting up a new market research function.
- Expanding your international business.
- Planning the construction of a new plant.
- Getting a new senior executive acclimated to the company.
- Restructuring your manufacturing operations to accommodate a new technology.
- Planning the launch of a new product line that takes you into a new market niche.
- Implementing a new work-at-home program.

In Summary: Implementation Planning

The major concepts of Implementation Planning are:

1. Formulate the Plan Statement
   - Develop

2. Identify Plan Objectives
   - Overall guidelines

3. Identify Plan Components
   - Decision Analyses
   - Tasks

- Actions
- List is never complete

4. Schedule Events and Times
    - What happens when?
    - Time pattern influences:
        Deadline dates
        Time windows
        Dependent relationships
    - Time increments
    - Who's responsible?

5. Revisit Components—Make Additional:
    - Decision Analyses
    - Sub-plans
    - Sub-sub-plans
    - Other models
    - Master plan?

6. Perform Objectives Test
    - Can they be met?
    - Resolve conflicts

7. Redraft the Plan
    - Periodic update

8. Perform Analysis Review
    - Actual vs. Planned

7

Potential Problem/Opportunity Analysis

Potential Problem Analysis focuses on looking for negative or undesirable Unplanned Future Change. Potential Opportunity Analysis focuses on looking for positive or desirable Unplanned Future Change. The objective of Potential Problem Analysis is to *prevent* unplanned negative change from happening. The objective of Potential Opportunity Analysis is to *promote* the occurrence of unplanned positive change.

You can use the tools of Potential Problem Analysis to accomplish two different goals. First, you can uncover things that could go wrong in the ongoing, supposedly routine conduct of the organization's affairs and then take steps to prevent them from happening. (In this mode, there are only minor differences between the Potential Problem Analysis approach and the Potential Opportunity Analysis approach.)

The second way of employing Potential Problem Analysis tools is to detect and prevent problems in conjunction with the implementation of a major Planned Future Change such as the launch of a new product, the start-up of a new plant or process, the set up of a new regional office. You will use the tools much more effectively in this mode if you have first developed an Implementation Plan as described in the previous chapter.

Although there are two ways to use the Potential Problem Analysis tools, Potential Opportunity Analysis's role is purely to uncover opportunities in the ongoing, routine conduct of business. You don't need to apply Potential

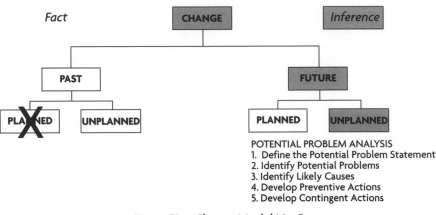

Figure 7.1   Change Model No. 5

Opportunity Analysis to an Implementation Plan because the plan itself defines the ideal happening, the opportunity itself; accomplishing 100% of the plan is the utopian outcome. There is no reason you can't apply Potential Opportunity Analysis to a plan, but from a practical and pragmatic standpoint—considering the effective use of your time and priorities—the potential is seldom there for significant return from such an effort. The issue in implementation is a Potential Problem Analysis concern of not achieving 100% of the plan, as opposed to a Potential Opportunity Analysis consideration of trying to exceed 100%.

Another way of looking at the uses of Potential Problem Analysis and Potential Opportunity Analysis involves macro and micro applications of Potential Problem Analysis and the macro application of Potential Opportunity Analysis. In this chapter, we'll explore micro Potential Problem Analysis, detecting potential problems in Implementation Plans (Figure 7.1). Macro Potential Problem Analysis and Potential Opportunity Analysis, uncovering problems and opportunities in ongoing organizational activities, are discussed in Chapter 11 on Potential Future Change.

Potential Problem Analysis—Micro

As depicted in Figure 7.1, the Potential Problem Analysis process has five steps:

1. Define the Potential Problem Statement
2. Identify Potential Problems
3. Identify Likely Causes
4. Develop Preventive Actions
5. Develop Contingent Actions

As in the other processes we've seen,

> Each step builds on, evolves from, depends on, the information developed in the preceding steps.

Step One: Define the Potential Problem Statement

By definition, the Potential Problem Statement is negative in tone; it's supposed to focus you on the downside. The problem solver does two things simultaneously in this statement: identifies potential future changes and casts negative value judgments on them. From the purist's perspective, this is undesirable; one should take things one step at a time: identify potential future changes first and then, second, determine if each is positive or negative. However, from a practical and pragmatic perspective, separating the two steps is seldom time and resource effective. It is most efficient to simply express the concern this way: "What could go wrong with?" The concern is easily derived from the Implementation Plan Statement. For example, if the Plan Statement is "Develop the best plan for getting our Salt Lake City regional office operational," then the Potential Problem Statement in its broadest form is "What could go wrong in the process of getting our Salt Lake City regional office operational?"

Sometimes you can get dumped into a Potential Problem Analysis concern that isn't linked to any Decision or Implementation Plan that you've been involved with. For example, suppose you've just become aware that Product X is going to be launched soon. Given your knowledge of what's happened in past new-product launches, you're wondering if all the things that could go wrong with the product once it's in use have been identified and prevented. In this case, your Potential Problem Statement can be derived from the upcoming event: "What could go wrong with Product X once it's launched?"

Or suppose you've just been named plant manager of a plant that's soon to undertake a major expansion. You could be concerned with whether or not the expansion will perform as expected when it's started up. If you decide to devote effort to this concern, your Potential Problem Statement might be "What could go wrong in our plant expansion when it's started up?"

Step Two: Identify Potential Problems

The Potential Problem Statement outlines the area in which you search for potential problems. To understand exactly how one goes about identifying them, let's start with a Potential Problem Analysis situation in which you're a newcomer to the scene—the launch of Product X, for example. The problem solvers need to look at the Potential Problem Statement "What could go wrong with Product X once it's launched?" and develop answers for that question.

Obviously one way to discover these answers is to open things up to a no-holds-barred fishing trip and allow anyone and everyone to express their thoughts. Although such an approach will usually generate a lengthy list, most of the items will likely be time-wasting trivia and, more important, will seldom contain the not-so-obvious potential problems that usually are the sources of big trouble.

Uncovering significant but hidden potential problems requires precise, directed, questioning that asks knowledgeable people (information sources) to look at the Potential Problem Statement in particular ways. The following are some questions that can identify more clearly the elements that could go wrong:

- What controllable actions, conditions, events is this dependent on?
- What uncontrollable actions, conditions, events is this dependent on?
- What other actions, conditions, events are dependent on this?
- In what ways is this new or different from how it was done, or the way it existed, before?
- What is based on inference, supposition, speculation?
- What is unchangeable, inflexible, locked in?
- Where is there little or no latitude or margin for error?

Another approach to uncovering potential problems requires first painting a picture of the basic fundamentals that underlie what is to be accomplished or implemented. You paint this picture by responding to the following questions:

- What function(s) is this supposed to accomplish, what output(s) is this supposed to deliver?
- What unneeded, undesirable functions or outputs accompany these?
- What input(s) or environment must be provided for these functions to be accomplished and these outputs delivered?
- What unneeded, undesirable inputs or environment accompany these?

Once this picture of the basic fundamentals has been painted, any failure to fulfill any one of the desired elements defines a potential problem.

Further, the unneeded or undesirable elements can be sources of potential problems. Thus this perspective offers a fertile field for potential problems.

When looking for potential problems, don't forget to identify and explore the *system* that surrounds and impinges on the Potential Problem Analysis area. This might be defined as embracing any factor, internal or external, that has the potential to be the source of something that could go wrong or affect the probability or seriousness of potential problems already identified.

If an Implementation Plan has been created, then the starting point for targeting specific potential problems is easy to find; all you have to do is go to your Plan Components list. Each potential failure to accomplish a component is a potential problem.

The Meeting

The problem solvers working on the Salt Lake City regional office referred to their Plan Components and came up with the following list of potential problems:

A. We don't get the part of the city selected on time.
B. We don't get the site selected and lease signed on time.
C. We don't determine what functions should be done regionally on time.
D. We don't get our employee staffing determined on time.
E. We don't have our printed materials available on time.
F. We don't get our employees moved on time.
G. We don't get our new employees hired on time.
H. We don't get our new employees properly trained on time.
I. We don't have appropriate communications lines operating properly on time.
J. We don't do a good job of properly notifying our southwest regional customers.
K. We don't have the equipment we need operational in time.
L. We don't correctly determine our space needs in time.

Each of these Potential Problem Statements is simply an expression of failure to accomplish the corresponding Plan Component in the intended manner.

Deciding Which Potential Problems to Pursue

Regardless of how you've approached it, you now have a lengthy list of potential problems staring you in the face; that's good and bad news. The good news is that you have the list. The bad news is that it's lengthy. However, in all likelihood many of these potential problems have a low probability of ever happening and some of them would probably have little impact even if they did occur?

Thus the simplest way to whittle down the list of potential problems identified to one to be pursued is to size up each potential problem against two measures: its probability of actually happening and its seriousness if it did. Practically speaking, judgments of high, medium, or low (H, M, or L) are usually completely adequate for this purpose since the objective is simply to select which potential problems to pursue and which to walk away from, forget about, or accept the risk on.

The whole raison d'etre of Potential Problem Analysis is that "an ounce of prevention is worth a pound of cure." However, this maxim assumes that the cure is worthwhile. Without an appropriate determination of which potential problems really have significance, it's possible to make the cure more expensive than the ill; one could expend more resources preventing the potential problems from happening than they would cost if they actually occurred.

For most problem solvers, any potential problem with a low probability (P = L) and a low seriousness (S = L) is one to forget about; others may choose to set the accept-the-risk (AR) bar even higher.

The Meeting

The Salt Lake City regional office problem solvers considered their latest Events and Times Worksheet and started discussing each potential problem in the worksheet's sequence.

- With regard to determining regional functions (Potential Problem C), they felt that this would not be difficult and, even if it was only partially completed on time, they would still be able to get employee staffing (D) underway on time.
- They believed the probability of not completing employee staffing (D) on time was low and, even if they didn't, they wouldn't be in a time crunch, thus the seriousness was low.
- Likewise, they thought determining equipment needs (K) would be easy to accomplish and had plenty of time cushion with it; ditto with determining space needs (L).
- Because of the timing, selecting the best part of the city (A), choosing the best building (B), and setting up phone lines (I) were all felt

to be low, low, as was notifying customers (J).

- Considering their printer's erratic performance in the past, they rated getting letterhead and forms printed up (E) as medium, medium.
- Because hiring local people (G) came up as medium, medium, they felt the same assessments had to be applied to training them (H).
- Given the tight timing on moving people to Salt Lake City (F), it warranted a medium and a high.
- Considering the low, low rankings, the team decided to accept the risk on potential problems A, B, C, D, I, J, K, and L.

Figure 7.2 shows how their potential problems list looked at this stage.

Step Three: Identify Likely Causes

To repeat: The rationale of Potential Problem Analysis is that "an ounce of prevention is worth a pound of cure." However, simply identifying potential problems doesn't in any way prevent them from happening. The only way potential problems can be prevented is to prevent their causes, their initiators, from ever happening. Thus the real payoff from Potential

PLAN/SITUATION STATEMENT: Develop the best plan for getting our Salt Lake City regional office operational			
POTENTIAL PROBLEMS	P	S	AR
A	We don't get the part of the city selected on time.	L	L	✔
B	We don't get the site selected and lease signed on time.	L	L	✔
C	We don't determine what functions should be done regionally on time.	L	L	✔
D	We don't get our employee staffing determined on time.	L	L	✔
E	We don't have our printed materials available on time.	M	M	
F	We don't get our employees moved on time.	M	H	
G	We don't get our new employees hired on time.	M	M	
H	We don't get our new employees properly trained on time.	M	M	
I	We don't have the appropriate communications lines operating properly on time.	L	L	✔
J	We don't do a good job of properly notifying our southwest regional customers on time.	L	L	✔
K	We don't have the equipment we need operational in time.	L	L	✔
L	We don't correctly determine our space needs in time.	L	L	✔

Figure 7.2   Potential Problems Worksheet

Problem Analysis comes from identifying the likely causes of the potential problems and then preventing them from occurring.

Once the problem solvers have gone through the grueling rigor of identifying potential problems, determining their likely causes usually isn't difficult. It's much easier than problem identification because each quest is much more precisely and narrowly focused and because it is parallel and sequential to the modus operandi of the potential problem identification.

Just as you need to focus on the significant potential problems and dump the trivial ones—by assessing their probability and seriousness—you must separate the wheat from the chaff as you examine likely causes. However, you need to assess likely causes *only* on their probability of happening or causing the potential problem. Likely causes in and of themselves have no individual seriousness; rather their seriousness is that of the problem they produce.

Now that we have discussed assessing the probability and seriousness of potential problems and the probability of likely causes, and have used probability and seriousness assessments to decide whether to further pursue or ignore a particular potential problem, there may be some purists who are on the verge of crying "Foul!" They may have spotted the (not so obvious?) question of "How can you judge the probability of a potential problem unless you have *first* anticipated each of its likely causes and their respective probabilities of happening?" The pure answer is you can't. The pragmatic answer is that it's a function of reasoned knowledge and competence.

If effective Potential Problem Analysis depended on first anticipating every potential problem and then every likely cause before whittling the list down to a workable size, there wouldn't be any such thing as effective Potential Problem Analysis. In short, the cure would be guaranteed to be more expensive than the ill before you even got started.

The Meeting

Here's where the Salt Lake City regional office problem solvers are at this stage. The team members developed likely causes for Potential Problem E, assessed the probability of each cause, and noted where they were going to accept the risk with the result as shown in Figure 7.3.

Several subtle yet important lessons can be learned from their likely causes. With regard to "We don't have our telephone numbers assigned in time," note that the group recognized that this cause could be stairstepped down to two further likely causes: "We don't apply for them in time" and "The phone company won't preassign them." Thus the first lesson is not to overlook the concept of stairstepping.

PLAN/SITUATION STATEMENT: Develop the best plan for getting our Salt Lake City regional office operational		
E	POTENTIAL PROBLEM: We don't have our printed materials available on time.	P M	S M
LIKELY CAUSES		P	AR
1	We don't have our site selected on time, and thus don't know the address.	L	✔
2	We don't have our telephone numbers assigned in time: a. We don't apply for them in time. b. The phone company won't preassign them.	L M	✔
3	We don't get the job to the printer on time.	L	✔
4	Our printer doesn't get the job done on time.	M	
5	We don't catch typographical mistakes on the printer's proof.	L	✔
6	The materials are lost in transit to Salt Lake City.	L	✔

Figure 7.3   Likely Causes Worksheet No. 1

Also, "We don't catch typographical mistakes on the printer's proofs" was originally worded "Our printer makes typographical mistakes" and was assigned a medium probability. However, someone in the group pointed out that the printer always furnishes proofs whenever changes are made and won't proceed until they are approved. Thus the likely cause was restated and the probability reassessed. The second lesson is the importance of precise, accurate wording for expressing the concern.

The team then moved on to the next potential problem, F, and developed the Likely Causes Worksheet shown in Figure 7.4.

The team also proceeded to develop likely causes and assess their probabilities for Potential Problems G and H.

Step Four: Develop Preventive Actions

The ultimate objective of Potential Problem Analysis is to ensure that nothing goes wrong in the course of the implementation of a decision or plan. The only way to maximize the probability of nothing going wrong is to

PLAN/SITUATION STATEMENT: Develop the best plan for getting our Salt Lake City regional office operational				
F	POTENTIAL PROBLEM: We don't get our employees moved on time.		P M	S H
LIKELY CAUSES			P	AR
1	An employee changes his or her mind at the last minute.		L	
2	A last-minute family emergency delays an employee's moving time.		L	✔
3	An employee's financial circumstances prevent him or her from buying a new house until the existing house was sold.		M	
4	The employee's new housing won't be available in time.		L	✔

5	A moving company doesn't live up to its promise:
	    a. Poor scheduling
	    b. Equipment breakdown
			M
			L
				
				 ✔

6	An employee can't find housing in Salt Lake City that is acceptable.		L	✔

Figure 7.4   Likely Causes Worksheet No. 2

minimize the probability of any potential problems occurring and, more specifically, prevent likely causes with unacceptable risk from happening. This is accomplished by undertaking specific actions designed to prevent a likely cause from ever seeing the light of day. Effective preventive actions will reduce the residual probabilities (RP)—the probability of the problem still occurring *after* the preventive action has been taken—of likely causes to low, thus in turn reducing the residual probability of the potential problem to low.

Too many would-be potential problem solvers drop the ball when they come to the Preventive Actions step. Whether through laziness or overinflated egos and self-confidence ("This is *my* plan, and nothing ever goes wrong with *my* plans"), they do a good job of developing a list of preventive actions and then never carry them out. Their defense is to mumble something like, "Well, the probabilities are probably overinflated anyway, and if the problems do occur, well, we'll undertake (preventive) actions at that time."

Please think intelligently and logically for a minute. When a potential problem actually happens, it can no longer be prevented and the preventive actions have instantaneously become worthless—along with the effort you devoted to Potential Problem Analysis up to that point.

The Meeting

Let's look in on the progress of the Salt Lake City team at this point (summarized in Figure 7.5). With regard to Potential Problem E, they decided to accept the risk of all the low probability likely causes. They then developed preventive actions for the two medium probability likely causes.

Notice that, in each case, they felt that the preventive action reduced the likely cause's probability to a residual probability (RP) of low. Thus the residual probability of the potential problem's happening would be low once the preventive actions had been taken.

Moving on to Potential Problem F, there was considerable discussion about whether to accept the risk of the low probability likely causes. Even though the probability of "An employee changes his or her mind . . ." was felt to be low, the group wasn't willing to accept the risk. They felt that, if this happened, the seriousness would go beyond the impact on the Salt Lake City office. They reasoned that the employee would probably feel guilty or ostracized or both and might even leave the company; thus they could lose a valued employee on top of having to deal with the Salt Lake City issue.

As far as the other low probability likely causes were concerned, they

PLAN/SITUATION STATEMENT: Develop the optimum plan for getting our Salt Lake City regional office operational					
E	POTENTIAL PROBLEM: We don't have our printed materials available on time.			P M	S M
LIKELY CAUSES		P	PREVENTIVE ACTIONS	WHO	RP
2 b	We don't have our telephone numbers assigned on time. The phone company won't preassign them.	M	Pay a nearby office to let us get the lines installed at their location *or* get them installed at the realtor's office (add this condition to the objectives used to select the realtor).	MCF	L
4	Our printer doesn't get the job done in time.	M	Have heart-to-heart talk with printer and if he won't agree to penalty clause, get new printer.	BAE	L

Figure 7.5   Actions Worksheet No. 1

PLAN/SITUATION STATEMENT: Develop the optimum plan for getting our Salt Lake City regional office operational					
F	POTENTIAL PROBLEM: We don't get our employees moved on time.			P M	S H
	LIKELY CAUSES	P	PREVENTIVE ACTIONS	WHO	RP
1	An employee changes his or her mind at the last minute and decides not to move.	L	Have counselor meet with each employee and spouse who are offered a transfer before they respond to the offer.	JWD	L
3	An employee's financial circumstances prevent him or her from buying a new house until the existing house was sold.	M	Offer no-interest down payment loan to be paid back within 60 days of sale of existing house; company buys existing house at average of three appraisals 60 days after move.	JWD	L
5 a	A moving company doesn't live up to its promise: Poor scheduling	M	Investigate all local movers' past year's moves and develop penalty clauses with acceptable ones.	ECW	L

Figure 7.6   Actions Worksheet No. 2

accepted their risk. This left them to develop the preventive actions indicated in Figure 7.6.

The group proceeded to develop preventive actions for the remainder of the likely causes with medium or high probability of happening.

Step Five: Develop Contingent Actions

When you create a list of potential problems, you assess the probability that each one will actually happen as well as the seriousness of it if it did. At this stage of the game you hope that all the medium and high probabilities you identified at the start have now had their residual probability reduced to low. But what about their seriousness?

The probabilities of the potential problems you identified are now all low, but are they zero? And what about the potential problem—or problems—that you never thought of or never identified that might have a medium or high probability of happening? What about a low probability, high seriousness potential problem that could threaten human life? Despite the supreme confidence you may have in your Potential Problem Analysis efforts thus far, only an imprudent person would ignore the potential problems that possess medium and high seriousness if they do occur. Thus the challenge now becomes thinking out specific contingent actions that would automatically be triggered if and when a specific potential problem happens so as to minimize its effects, its seriousness. There are two key elements to developing effective contingent actions: first, developing the action itself, and, second, developing and setting up its trigger mechanism.

When you get to the point of thinking about contingent actions, your focus is solely on the Potential Problem Statement, on minimizing the problem's seriousness if and when it happens. Forget about your list of likely causes—they have no relevance; the potential problem could happen because of a likely cause that you never thought of, because of a less than effective preventive action, or whatever. A contingent action should minimize the effects of the problem *regardless* of what caused it.

Also, don't forget that contingent actions are worthless unless they cut in the instant that the problem hits. Therefore, it's imperative to nail down the trigger when the contingent action is defined as well as determine who is responsible for monitoring the situation.

The Meeting

When the Salt Lake City regional office team members addressed contingent actions, they first tackled Potential Problem E, indicated in Figure 7.7.

PLAN/SITUATION STATEMENT: Develop the optimum plan for getting our Salt Lake City regional office operational				
E	POTENTIAL PROBLEM: We don't have our printed materials available on time.		P M	S M
LIKELY CAUSES		P	PREVENTIVE ACTIONS	WHO	RP
2 b	We don't have our telephone numbers assigned on time. The phone company won't preassign them.	M	Pay a nearby office to let us get the lines installed at their location *or* get them installed at the realtor's office (add this condition to the objectives used to select the realtor).	MCF	L
4	Our printer doesn't get the job done in time.	M	Have heart-to-heart talk with printer and if he won't agree to penalty clause, get new printer.	BAE	L
	CONTINGENT ACTION: Identify labels that could be printed and placed on our headquarter materials. Get type set for printing them. Identify quick printer who can produce them on short notice.		TRIGGER: 1. Call the printer one week before materials are due. If he's not going to meet delivery date, initiate Contingent Action *or* 2. Failure of materials to be received on due date.	WHO BAE

Figure 7.7   Actions Worksheet No. 3

Going back to their Plan Statement (Chapter 6), they noted that Betty would be the person responsible for monitoring this situation.

The team then moved on to Potential Problem F, shown in Figure 7.8.

Conduct Analysis Review

After the mission for which the Potential Problem Analysis was done has been accomplished, a sixth step should be undertaken to encourage even more effective Potential Problem Analysis in the future; this step involves learning from experience.

While the events are fresh in everyone's mind, all those involved in the Potential Problem Analysis effort should meet to examine what actually happened against the documentation. If any contingent actions were

PLAN/SITUATION STATEMENT: Develop the optimum plan for getting our Salt Lake City regional office operational					
F	POTENTIAL PROBLEM: We don't get our employees moved on time.			P M	S H
LIKELY CAUSES		P	PREVENTIVE ACTIONS	WHO	RP
1	An employee changes his or her mind at the last minute and decides not to move.	L	Have counselor meet with each employee and spouse who are offered a transfer before they respond to the offer.	JWD	L
3	An employee's financial circumstances prevent him or her from buying a new house until he or she has sold his or her existing house.	M	Offer no-interest down payment loan to be paid back within 60 days of sale of existing house; company buys existing house at average of three appraisals 60 days after move.	JWD	L
5 a	A moving company doesn't live up to its promise: Poor scheduling	M	Investigate all local movers' past year's moves and develop penalty clauses with acceptable ones.	ECW	L
	CONTINGENT ACTION: Designate an emergency backup headquarters employee for each person being moved and have these backup persons available to fly to Salt Lake City within 24-hours notice.		TRIGGER: Employee hasn't left for Salt Lake City four days before office start-up date or hasn't arrived at Salt Lake City two days before.	WHO JWD	

Figure 7.8   Actions Worksheet No. 4

required, did they work as intended—if not, why? If contingent actions were required, by definition it was because preventive actions didn't work, likely causes weren't anticipated, probabilities were assessed too low, or combinations of these factors. This is where the real learning about how to do better Potential Problem Analysis takes place—dig into what actually happened and find out why. (If no contingent actions were required, then by definition everything went well; thus there may not be anything to learn from an analysis review.)

The World of Potential Problem Analysis

You've just gone through an in-depth illustration of the application of the Potential Problem Analysis tools to a plan to start up a new office. But there's a wide world of other types of Unplanned Future Change situations out there in which this thinking process can be used. For example:

- Identify and prevent things that could go wrong in the launch of a product in foreign markets.
- Uncover and prevent the hidden problems in a new plant before it is started up.
- Detect the troubles that could arise in an overseas acquisition and determine how to prevent them.
- Analyze how a major competitor with significant new funding will try to attack your market positions and how its efforts could be derailed.
- Uncover and eliminate the unexpected problems in a major process redesign that involves technology that has never been used before in this manner.
- Determine and prevent the problems that could arise in setting up a new joint venture overseas.
- Describe and determine how to prevent the problems that could surface when merging two organizations with major functions that duplicate each other.
- Uncover and prevent the problems that could arise as customers adopt a product that depends on a technology most of them aren't familiar with.

In Summary: Potential Problem Analysis

The major concepts of Potential Problem Analysis are:

1. Define the Potential Problem Statement
   - What could go wrong?

2. Identify Potential Problems
   - What is this dependent on?
   - What depends on this?
   - How is this different?
   - Speculation, inflexible?
   - No margin for error?
   - Probability and seriousness

3. Identify Likely Causes
   - What could cause this?
   - Probability

4. Develop Preventive Actions
   - Remove likely causes
   - Reduce probability
   - Residual probability

5. Develop Contingent Actions
   - Reduce seriousness
   - Trigger, who?

6. Conduct Analysis Review
   - Contingent Actions
     - Did they work?
     - Why were they needed?

8

Problem Analysis

The Decision Analysis tools provide a structured thinking process for dealing with Planned Future Change. The Potential Problem Analysis tools provide a structured thinking process for dealing with Unplanned Future Change. Now it's time to explore the last type of change, Unplanned Past Change (Figure 8.1) and develop the structured thinking process called Problem Analysis. It is a thinking process for finding the cause of such concerns as: "Excessive employee turnover" and "Short life of Component X."

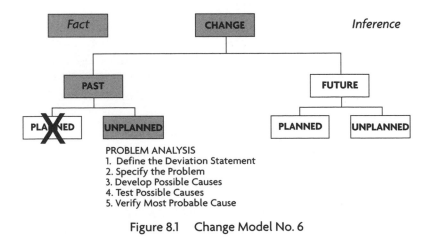

Figure 8.1   Change Model No. 6

As depicted in Figure 8.1, there are five conceptual steps in the Problem Analysis process:

1. Define the Deviation Statement
2. Specify the Problem
3. Develop Possible Causes
4. Test Possible Causes
5. Verify Most Probable Cause

Step One: Define the Deviation Statement

The first step in Problem Analysis is to define the Deviation Statement. The term Deviation Statement is preferred to Problem Statement because, in discussing Unplanned Past Change, problems *are* deviations. Indeed, in examining the structural differences and thus the thinking approach differences between problems and decisions, Kepner and Tregoe[1] and Herbert Simon[2] have, with their own variations on the wording, defined "problem" as:

> **A situation in which what is actually happening has deviated from what should be happening.**

At this point we're abandoning the generic use of the word "problem" and focusing on the more precise definition developed by Kepner-Tregoe and Simon. The word "deviation" accurately and precisely defines what the required statement must describe to set up the subsequent steps.

When we talk about an Unplanned Past Change, we are saying that what is presently being experienced has not only changed from what was previously experienced, but has also deviated—has departed—from a known condition or standard or norm, from what should be happening. Thus the difference between what should be happening and what is actually happening defines the deviation (Figure 8.2).

In examining Figure 8.2, note that a deviation can be either positive or negative, desirable or undesirable. Regardless of whether the yield in a manufacturing process has dropped below the norm or risen above it or whether sales have fallen or increased dramatically, the problem solvers want to know why—they want to find the cause. In the first (negative) case, they want to determine the cause so that they can remove it, correct things, and get back to the norm. In the second (positive) case, they want to find the cause so they can perpetuate it and define and maintain a new norm, a new should.

Thus a Deviation Statement is simply the difference between what is actually happening and what should be happening:

Should − Actual = Deviation

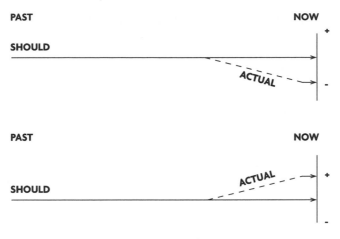

Figure 8.2   Deviation Diagram No. 1

You may also encounter a situation in which actual performance fluctuates widely and yet the fluctuations are acceptable; they are within the *band* of the norm, the should. Such a situation is shown in the Acceptable Deviation Diagram in Figure 8.3. However, changing circumstances may subsequently dictate that the band of the should must be narrowed. When this is the case, you need to find the causes of the fluctuations so that they can be eliminated by taking action against them. Using the Problem Analysis tools, simply pick a pair of adjacent high and low spots—shown as A and B in Figure 8.3—and do a Problem Analysis on them to find the cause of that specific deviation. Once that cause is known, you can then analyze B and C, D and E, and so on in the same fashion.

An Example

When I reviewed my experiences with Problem Analysis situations to find

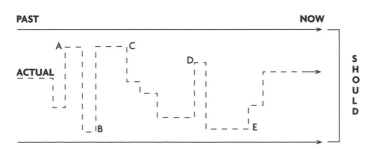

Figure 8.3   Acceptable Deviation Diagram

an example to use to illustrate the Problem Analysis tools, my main objective was to select one that was simple, neat, straightforward, and easy to understand and follow through the steps. Guess what? I couldn't find any that met that objective.

Since the example was going to be disguised anyway, my first thought was to reconstruct one to make it simple. However, the more I thought about that, the more I realized this would be a disservice to someone who really wants to become proficient at Problem Analysis. It would make the process appear to be much easier than it really is.

Problem Analysis is a much more difficult process to master than Decision Analysis and Potential Problem Analysis for two reasons. First, Decision Analysis and Potential Problem Analysis deal with inferential information—there are no right and wrong answers to the questions asked in using these processes, no black and white, only shades of gray. Problem Analysis entails factual information; the answers to the questions asked in Problem Analysis are either right or wrong, black or white. Consequently, the tools of Problem Analysis are less forgiving than those of Decision Analysis and Potential Problem Analysis.

The second reason Problem Analysis is more difficult is that most problem situations deal with something that has gone wrong. Time, money, materials, products, or whatever are being lost and the pressure is on to do something—now! Thus, many would-be problem solvers are all too prone to jump to quick conclusions and make assumptions about the cause without first taking time to understand the facts surrounding the problem.

Unfortunately, once people come up with pet ideas, their egos often become invested and they will cling steadfastly to those ideas. If and when subsequent facts about the problem shoot holes in them, they will often repeatedly amend the ideas with "Yes, but . . ." assumptions. Thus, the person who wants to pursue a clean, neat Problem Analysis process has to invest considerable time and effort in getting the excuse and assumption makers on track and keeping them there. How? By sticking rigorously to the Problem Analysis process and using the questions in each step of the process to determine the relevance of the information provided by each source.

As you will see, the example that was selected is *not* simple, neat, or straightforward. However, it is a realistic example of the kind of situation that the problem solver can face on the job. The supporting explanation should make it easy to understand and follow the steps. It certainly will illustrate the mental agility and belief in the process that one needs to become successful with Problem Analysis.

The example involves a company that manufactures exotic metal alloys in powder form—let's call it Alloys, Inc. Several of its customers had found a new application for a proprietary product it had recently launched and the sales of this product, Alloy 123, were growing rapidly. Everything was going well until one day when Quality Control started rejecting almost half of what was being manufactured. Alloy 123 had a unique color that was critical to this new application, and the color coming out of manufacturing was far off target. Indeed, they had a problem.

Just as in Decision Analysis and Potential Problem Analysis, the initial statement of the situation becomes the focal point for the next step; it acts as the target of many questions that will define and add dimension to the problem. The essence of the effort to define a Deviation Statement is the old KISS dictum: Keep It Short and Simple. All it takes is a few words to define the target statement concisely for your questioning.

The should was that the product's color should be light green. The actual was that much of it was ranging from dark blue to black. Thus the Deviation Statement was:

Off-color product

Why not say "Dark blue to black Alloy 123?" True, that would be a more precise statement, but there can be a downside to investing too much effort in creating a detailed Deviation Statement at this stage. The Deviation Statement can end up starting to specify the problem—which is the next step. If you stretch out a Deviation Statement and end up with just one word of inaccurate information in it, the rest of the Problem Analysis can be thrown off track. Don't run that risk!

Now let's proceed with developing the next step of the Problem Analysis process.

Step Two: Specify the Problem

Every problem, regardless of what type it is, has four fundamental dimensions or characteristics that define what the problem Is:

1. It has an *identity*; it has information that describes *what* is happening.
2. It has a *location*; it has information that defines *where* it is happening.
3. It has a *timing*; it has information that defines *when* it is happening.
4. It has a *magnitude*; it has information that defines its *extent*.

Regardless of the type of problem, there is specific factual information that answers each of these four questions. However, in some problem situations, it's possible that some of these facts may not be immediately—or ever—available. For example, the pressure on the boiler the instant before it blew up was a fact, but if the gauge was destroyed or can't be found, we don't know what that pressure was. The Problem Analysis process is designed to deal with factual information, but in some cases the facts may not be available no matter how much exploration, question asking, or research you do. In such situations, the problem solver may be forced to substitute "best guesses" for facts. There's nothing wrong with making the best of a bad situation by doing this—so long as you *never* forget or ignore that you made the substitution. The best way to ensure that you remember is to put a big question mark next to each best guess.

In addition to the information that describes and defines the four dimensions of what, where, when, and extent, every problem also has information that describes and defines circumstances closely related to the problem but *not* a part of it. This information defines:

1. *What* else could have happened but didn't?
2. *Where* else could the problem have occurred but didn't?
3. *When* else could the problem have happened but didn't?
4. *What* could the *extent* of the problem have been but wasn't?

If you're going to fully understand the problem and its scope, as well as accurately define it and draw a boundary around it, then you must know this Is Not information as well.

The best way to paint a picture of the problem's dimensions is to set up a simple matrix as shown in Figure 8.4.

Repeatedly throughout the conceptual discussions thus far, the importance of effective questioning as the means for drawing out relevant information has been illustrated and stressed. This holds true in Problem Analysis as well. And each of the what, where, when, and extent dimensions actually has two separate pieces:

	IS	IS NOT
WHAT		
WHERE		
WHEN		
EXTENT		

Figure 8.4   Problem Specification Matrix No. 1

1. *What defect* is present, and what defects are not present?
   What object (item, person, etc.) is experiencing the defect, and what objects are not? (In "people problems," the object(s) may be particular persons.)
2. *Where* is the defect *observed* (in what geographic or other location), and where is it not observed?
   Where is the defect on the object, and where on the object is it not present?
3. *When* is the defect *observed* (clock or calendar time), and when is it not observed?
   When does the defect appear *on the object* (when in its life cycle), and when does it not appear?
   Note: Many problem solvers have difficulty understanding this *when on the object* concept. Look at it this way—every object goes through a life cycle. An automobile starts out as a frame; as it moves through the plant, parts are added to it along the way. It's then painted, shipped to a dealer, and subsequently sold. It's then driven and ultimately scrapped. That entire process constitutes an automobile's life cycle. A particular problem is likely to be specific to one or more parts of a life cycle.
4. What is the *extent* of the total problem, and what is it not (*how many* objects are/are not involved)?
   What is the *extent* of the individual defect, and what is it not (*how bad* is the defect)?

For purposes of simplicity, each of these questions was worded in the singular form. However, in some problems the plural many be appropriate—there may be multiple defects, objects, locations, or times involved. However, let me throw in one *huge* caution at this point. If, as you start to analyze your problem, you find that multiple defects are present or multiple objects or locations or times are involved, step back and objectively ask yourself whether you're looking at only one problem or if you are attempting to combine several problems into one. Often problem solvers—consciously or subconsciously—attempt to combine several problems into one, thinking that it will make the analysis easier. Nothing could be further from the truth. At best, combining problems will make finding their individual causes much more difficult; at worst, it will make it impossible.

When in doubt, attack each instance of each dimension individually. The worst that can happen is that you'll find that the cause for your initial problem also fits the second, the third, and so on. If this is the case, you'll discover it in record time.

The Example

The Off-Color Product Problem Matrix of Figure 8.5 shows the outcome of Alloys, Inc.'s problem specification.

There are several lessons to be learned from this problem's specification. First, recall the need to exercise caution when you see multiple defects, objects, locations, or times involved in a problem. Is this specification really *one* problem or could there be several separate problems lumped together? Although there are multiple objects (lot numbers) and times involved here, the fact that they all relate to one defect and one product suggests that the problem probably involves multiple occurrences of the same cause. Nevertheless, the problem analysts here had to remain aware that this assumption could subsequently prove incorrect.

DEVIATION STATEMENT: Off-color Product		
	IS	IS NOT
WHAT		
Defect	Off-color product	Poor physical properties
Object	Alloy 123	Any other product
	Lots 147	Lots 146, 145
	144–141	140, 139
	138	137–129
	128–125	124–118
	117–112	111–100
	99–91	90–86
	85	84–82
	81	80–01
WHERE		
Observed	Line 7	Other lines
	After hydrogen treatment	Before
On object	Particle surface	Uniformly through particle
	Entire surface	Part of surface
WHEN		
Observed	Nov. 15	Nov. 14 & 13
	10–7	6 & 3
	2	1–Oct. 20
	Oct. 19–16	Oct. 13–5
	4– Sept. 27	Sept. 26–11
	Sept. 8–Aug. 28	Aug. 25–21
	Aug. 18	Aug. 17–15
	14	11 or before
On object	After hydrogen treatment	Before
EXTENT		
How bad	Dark blue to black	Light green, other colors
How many	Approx. 40% of lots	Standard = 0%, over 40%
	25% to 100% of a lot	Less than 25%

Figure 8.5   Off-Color Product Problem Matrix No. 1

Second, notice that this problem existed, on and off, for three months before this Problem Analysis was started. Whenever you get involved with a problem that's over a few *minutes* old, you can bet that people have already made changes in the conditions surrounding the problem in a vain attempt to get rid of it. These well-intentioned efforts could have seriously distorted the problem's conditions and damaged the information, the true specification of the problem. (During these three months, the company's engineers and scientists had spent countless hours twisting knobs and changing dials in a futile effort to eliminate the problem. Finally top management called a screeching halt to their internal problem-solving efforts and asked for help.)

Seeing such a lengthy when dimension should automatically be a red flag that tells you to find out what these changes were *before* you go any further because they may make it necessary to redraw the problem's dimensions and to change the specification.

As soon as you see this red flag, stop and ask everyone involved what actions they've already taken and when each one was taken. The following is a list of changes that people had made along the way in an attempt to "solve" the off-color problem and the dates when each action was taken.

Changes made in the Alloy 123 manufacturing process:

1. Increased temperature of hydrogen treatment (Aug. 30)
2. Decreased temperature of hydrogen treatment (Aug. 31)
3. Increased pressure of hydrogen treatment (Sept. 1)
4. Decreased pressure of hydrogen treatment (Sept. 5)
5. Increased duration of hydrogen treatment (Sept. 6)
6. Decreased duration of hydrogen treatment (Sept. 7)
7. Changed hydrogen tanks (Sept. 8)
8. Changed hydrogen treatment containers (Sept. 29)
9. Changed cleaning process for containers (Oct. 3)
10. Cleaned hydrogen treatment chamber (Oct. 4)
11. Stopped blending (Oct. 5)
12. Installed new piping and valves to chamber (Oct. 21)
13. Decreased quantity of material in a lot (Nov. 3)

When you see such a lengthy and erratic when dimension, it can often be helpful, particularly in subsequent steps, to convert the time span into a separate, chronological listing, as shown in Figure 8.6. While you're at it, note on the listing when each of the actions was taken.

Date	Lot	Action	Date	Lot	Action
Nov. 15	**147***		Sept. 29	**114**	Changed hydrogen treatment containers
14	146		28	**113**	
13	145		27	**112**	
10	**144**		26	111	
9	**143**		25	110	
8	**142**		22	109	
7	**141**		21	108	
6	140		20	107	
3	139	Decreased quantity in lot	19	106	
2	**138**		18	105	
1	137		15	104	
Oct. 31	136		14	103	
30	135		13	102	
27	134		12	101	
26	133		11	100	
25	132		8	**99**	Changed hydrogen tanks
24	131		7	**98**	Decreased hydrogen treatment duration
23	130		6	**97**	Increased hydrogen treatment duration
21		New hydrogen piping	5	**96**	Decreased hydrogen treatment pressure
20	129		1	**95**	Increased hydrogen treatment pressure
19	**128**		Aug. 31	**94**	Decreased hydrogen treatment temperature
18	**127**		30	**93**	Increased hydrogen treatment temperature
17	**126**		29	**92**	
16	**125**		28	**91**	
13	124		25	90	
12	123		24	89	
11	122		23	88	
10	121		22	87	
9	120		21	86	
6	119		18	**85**	
5	118	Stopped blending	17	84	
4	**117**	Cleaned hydrogen chamber	16	83	
3	**116**	Changed container cleaning	15	82	
2	**115**		14	**81**	

*__Bold__ lot numbers indicate off-color lots.

Figure 8.6   Off-Color Problem Chronology

Choosing the Time Frame

The third lesson to be learned from this example is to first deal with a limited time frame. Alloys, Inc.'s problem analysts initially ignored the lot number and date information *after* lot 81 and August 14, respectively. The critical data they pursued in their quest for the cause—in the next step—were in the demarcation between lot 81 and lots 1 to 80, the demarcation between August 14 and all of Alloy 123's prior history. Thus, in their initial cut at Problem Analysis, they reduced the problem's dimension as shown in Figure 8.7, the Off-Color Product Problem Matrix No. 2.

There's one more lesson to be learned relative to specifying a long-standing problem that has absolutely nothing to do with the off-color product example. However, because of what we just did to the when dimension of the off-color product problem, it's appropriate to discuss it at this point. Suppose that you are working on a problem that produces an Is–Is Not picture similar to that shown in the Paper Company Problem Matrix in Figure 8.8.

A look at the when dimension in this specification shows you that the

DEVIATION STATEMENT: Off-color product		
	IS	IS NOT
WHAT		
Defect	Off-color product	Poor physical properties
Object	Alloy 123 Lot 81	Any other product Lots 80–01
WHERE		
Observed	Line 7 After hydrogen treatment	Other lines Before
On object	Particle surface Entire surface	Uniformly through particle Part of surface
WHEN		
Observed	Aug. 14	Aug. 11 or before
On object	After hydrogen treatment	Before
EXTENT		
How bad	Dark blue to black	Light green, other colors
How many	Approx. 40% of lots 25% to 100% of a lot	Standard = 0%, over 40% Less than 25%

Figure 8.7   Off-Color Product Problem Matrix No. 2

DEVIATION STATEMENT: Excessive holes in sheet		
	IS	IS NOT
WHAT		
Defect	Holes in sheet	Wrinkles, tears, etc.
Object	40# coated	Other grades
WHERE		
Observed	#3 paper machine First blade	#1 or #2 paper machine Other locations
On object	Front and back of sheet	Center
WHEN		

Observed	Mar. 15
	        10–7
	        2
	Feb. 19–16
	        4–Jan. 27
	Jan. 10–Dec. 28
	        11 PM to 11 AM
		Mar. 14–11
		        6–3
		        1–Feb. 20
		Feb. 15–5
		Jan. 26–11
		
		Other times

	Much the same all last year	
On object	At first blade	Before
EXTENT		
How bad	Often causes sheet to break	Acceptable
How many	Up to 5 a day	1 per day or less = norm

Figure 8.8   Paper Company Problem Matrix No. 1

problem is erratic and has been around for a long time. However here, unlike in the off-color product problem, there doesn't appear to be any unique starting point. The last thing you want to do, at the beginning at least, is to get tangled up in the whole problem, in all the dates. In this case, start your analysis by working only with the *latest* Is–Is Not time window (March 15 versus March 14–11). Take it all the way through and, when you find the cause, test it against each preceding when Is–Is Not pair; because different Is periods could have different causes.

The reason for working with the most recent time period is that in the critical subsequent steps—looking for differences and changes—the key information needed often comes out of people's heads, out of their mental data banks, not from log books or written records or computer printouts. The more recent the data, the more likely people are to remember them. If you don't find the cause working with the March 15 versus March 14–11 time window, then move back to the next time window (March 10–7 versus March 6–3) and start anew.

You have the message! Separate lengthy or cyclic problems into bite-size pieces; failure to do so can lead to indigestion.

Step Three: Develop Possible Causes

After having done the best job you can of filling in the Is–Is Not information—including marking every best guess with a red question mark—you're now staring at two families of information: Problem Is and Problem Is Not (Figure 8.9).

Obviously, there must be a reason why the information in the left column of your problem specification defines the problem and the information in the right column—which is closely related to the problem—is not a part of it. In some way, shape, or form, the information bounded by the left column is different from that in the right column—and therein lies the path to finding the cause of the problem.

	IS	IS NOT
WHAT		
WHERE	PROBLEM IS	PROBLEM IS NOT
WHEN		
EXTENT		

Figure 8.9   Problem Specification Matrix No. 2

To develop possible causes, you need to look at each Is–Is Not contrasting information pair and note what is different or distinctive about the Is piece compared to its companion Is Not piece. But before you proceed, this task can be simplified. *Invariably* the key difference—what leads to the cause—will be found in an Is–Is Not pair in which there's a sharp, decisive contrast between the two pieces of information. *Usually* this sharp contrast will be found in the responses to the what object, where observed, or when observed questions. (The value of the "sharp contrast" concept will become more evident when we get back to the Problem Analysis example.)

You have now expanded the Problem Specification Matrix to three columns, as shown in Figure 8.10.

The question to be applied to each of the sharp contrast Is–Is Not pairs is:

In what way(s) is the (Is) different from the (Is Not)?

Ask the question and plug the answer(s) into the third column. But beware, if there truly is a *real* difference, it will usually be quickly obvious. Do *not* linger and ponder the question if an obvious difference doesn't arise. This is a place where problem solvers can be prone to inventing or fabricating information. If a would-be problem solver has a pet idea about the cause, he or she will often go to great lengths to conjure up a nonexistent difference that will support that idea.

The Example

The problem analysts working on the off-color product examined the Is–Is Not information pairs for sharp contrast and targeted those pairs shown in the Off-Color Product Problem Matrix No. 3 (Figure 8.11) with an asterisk (*) between them. Remember, all this sharp contrast says is that "this ought to be a good place to look for differences"; it doesn't imply that you'll always find a difference for each sharp-contrast pair.

	IS	IS NOT	DIFFERENCES
WHAT			
WHERE			
WHEN			
EXTENT			

Figure 8.10   Problem Specification Matrix No. 3

DEVIATION STATEMENT: Off-color product			
	IS	IS NOT	DIFFERENCES
WHAT Defect Object 	Off-color product Alloy 123 . Lot 81	Poor physical properties * Any other product * Lots 80–01	 Hydrogen treatment Pulverizing method
WHERE Observed On object	Line 7 After hydrogen treatment Particle surface Entire surface	* Other lines Before Uniformly through particle Part of surface	Eutetic alloy raw material Hydrogen treatment Pulverizers Blender Argon chamber Operators Location
WHEN Observed On object	Aug. 14 After hydrogen treatment	* Aug. 11 or before Before	
EXTENT How bad How many	Dark blue to black Approx. 40% of lots 25% to 100% of a lot	Light green, other colors Standard = 0%, over 40% Less than 25%	

Figure 8.11   Off-Color Product Problem Matrix No. 3

Each entry in the differences column adds *new information* to the problem specification. Looking at the "where on the object" entries and seeing that the problem Is on the "particle surface" and Is Not "uniformly through particle," an overzealous (or underconfident) problem solver might be prone to write "surface phenomenon" in the corresponding differences column, for example. But this doesn't add new information; it doesn't tell the problem analysts anything they don't already know—all it does is restate the Is in different words.

Identifying Changes from Differences

The differences column is the raw material source in the quest for the cause. However, many of the differences will have existed since day one, since you first started business, since you first launched the product line, or

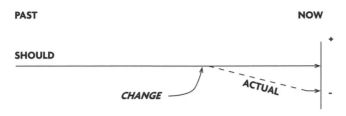

Figure 8.12   Deviation Diagram No. 2

whatever. But your problem hasn't existed since day one; it began only recently. Therefore, something had to change. Look at Deviation Diagram No. 2, as shown in Figure 8.12. Obviously, at the point where the actual departed from the should, something had to change. And therein lies the final truth in the quest for cause: cause comes from change. But the bottom line is that there are dozens of changes taking place in your environment every day; the only ones that you care about are those that have relevance to the problem. And those are the changes that happened in the information in the differences column. So now a fourth column needs to be added to the Problem Specification Matrix No. 4 (Figure 8.13). You then need to proceed to ask the question:

What, if anything, has changed in this difference?

In the when dimension, something that is different between an Is and an Is Not is something that changed at that point. The when dimension records information about a problem's timing; time doesn't stand still—it is constantly changing. Therefore, something that is different between two points in time, between an Is–Is Not information pair, is something that changed at the interface between those two points. Thus differences and changes are synonymous in the when dimension. Looking at the differences and

	IS	IS NOT	DIFFERENCES	CHANGES (TIMING)
WHAT				
WHERE				
WHEN				
EXTENT				

Figure 8.13   Problem Specification Matrix No. 4

DEVIATION STATEMENT: Excessive holes in sheet	IS	IS NOT	DIFFERENCES	CHANGES (TIMING)
WHAT Defect Object	Holes in sheet 40# coated	Wrinkles, tears, etc. Other grades	Pulp composition Coating	New formula (Feb. 10)
WHERE Observed	#3 paper machine First blade	#1 or #2 paper machine Other locations	Only makes coated sheet First place sheet gets higher tension	
On object	Front and back of sheet	Center	Sheet is dryer	
WHEN Observed	Mar. 15 10–7 2 Feb. 19–16 4–Jan. 27 Jan. 10–Dec. 28	Mar. 14–11 6–3 1–Feb. 20 Feb. 15–5 Jan. 26–11	Pulp composition ? ? ? ?	Pulp composition (Mar. 14, 10:38 PM)
	11 PM to 11 AM	Other times	Operators	Operators (4 PM, midnight, 8 AM)
	Much the same all last year			
On object	At first blade	Before	Higher tension on sheet	
EXTENT How bad How many	Often causes sheet to break Up to 5 a day	Acceptable 1 per day or less = norm		

Figure 8.14   Paper Company Problem Matrix No. 2

changes in the when dimension of the paper company problem provides an example of this (Figure 8.14).

As you write down changes, be sure to note *when* each change happened because this information will be important for the next step. Also, don't overlook the fact that all changes are not necessarily step changes (i.e., things that make an abrupt, instantaneous shift). Often changes will creep along slowly over a period of time; thus some changes may occur over a window or a span of time.

It's important here to raise another huge caution flag. In most cases, once you start looking for change in a difference, any change that really happened will usually pop out and be obvious. This step is a danger point in that it's a place where problem solvers can again be prone to inventing information or fabricating hypothetical change that never happened.

A related caution must also be raised at this point. In a problem such as the off-color product that has had the attention of many people for a long time, and which most likely involves working with a problem-solving team, as you proceed through the Develop Possible Causes step you'll often be faced with people throwing in their pet ideas about the cause. Most, if not all, of these will be off-the-wall whims that have no relevance to the question you're asking. An easy way of dealing with these outbursts—and of keeping things in the proper perspective—is to simply ask: "What question does that answer?" If it does answer a legitimate Develop Possible Causes question, use it—if it doesn't, pass it by and move on. However, if the pet-cause-pushers are persistent, put their ideas on a separate list; they can always be tested—and most likely shot down—later.

The Example

Off-Color Product Problem Matrix No. 4 (Figure 8.15) is the matrix that resulted when the problem analysts at Alloys, Inc., applied the change question to the information in their differences column. As you can see, the problem-solving team was able to find only one change. It discovered that the pressure regulator on the argon chamber had been replaced over the weekend. The changes the would-be problem solvers made after the problem started—listed earlier—were all after-the-fact changes that had no relevance to the problem the team was focusing on.

The next step was to hypothesize just how the change could have caused the problem and to develop a Possible Cause Statement. The statement the team developed said:

DEVIATION STATEMENT: Off-color product

	IS	IS NOT	DIFFERENCES	CHANGES (TIMING)
WHAT				
Defect	Off-color product	Poor physical properties	Hydrogen treatment	
Object	Alloy 123	Any other product	Pulverizing method	
	Lot 81	Lots 80–01		
WHERE				
Observed	Line 7	Other lines	Eutetic alloy raw material	New pressure regulator (Aug. 12)
			Hydrogen treatment	
			Pulverizers	
			Blender	
			Argon chamber	
	After hydrogen treatment	Before	Operators	
			Location	
On object	Particle surface	Uniformly through particle		
	Entire surface	Part of surface		
WHEN				
Observed	Aug. 14	Aug. 11 or before		
On object	After hydrogen treatment	Before		
EXTENT				
How bad	Dark blue to black	Light green, other colors		
How many	Approx. 40% of lots	Standard = 0%, over 40%		
	25% to 100% of a lot	Less than 25%		

Figure 8.15   Off-Color Product Problem Matrix No. 4

"Greater or lesser argon pressure is affecting the color of Alloy 123."

The possible cause then had to be tested to determine if it was valid.

Step Four: Test Possible Causes

Possible causes are just that—they're only possibilities until they have been unequivocally proven to be valid and shown to conform to *all* the facts of the problem specification. Thus the Problem Analysis process, specifically the Is and Is Not elements of the specification, provides a built-in testing ground for the fourth step: the examination of possible causes.

Again, effective questioning is the name of the game. The question to be applied here is:

If (Possible Cause) is the cause, how does it explain why the problem is (Is) and not (Is Not)?

In using this question, each pair of Is–Is Not information entries is plugged into the respective (Is) and (Is Not) blanks in the question. Starting at the top of your Is–Is Not columns, keep applying the question against successive pairs of Is–Is Not information entries so long as there are plausible answers. If you get to an Is–Is Not pair in which there clearly isn't any fit or any plausible explanation, then that possible cause is dead. Note where it died and move on to testing the next possible cause.

When testing a possible cause, you may come to a "shade of gray" situation, one in which a seemingly plausible possible cause isn't completely shot down but has a reasonable doubt raised about it. If this happens, look at the Is–Is Not pair where the doubt has been raised. Is there a difference between that pair that, when combined with the change, could explain the problem? If so, restate the Possible Cause Statement to include the difference and continue testing. Although cause *must* come from change, sometimes the change will produce the problem *only* in the presence of a difference. When this is the case, the testing process will lead you to it by raising a doubt at the point where the difference exists.

For example, in the paper company problem one possible cause came from the pulp composition change at 10:38 P.M. on March 14. However, that possible cause didn't explain why the problem occurred in the 11 P.M. to 11 A.M. period. Looking in the differences column of that Is–Is Not pair (11 P.M. to 11 A.M.–other times) reveals that the operators are different. Thus the possible cause was redefined to include the pulp composition change plus the different operators. (Without going into the details of the actual situation, it was found that this was the cause.)

If a doubt is raised by an Is–Is Not pair where no such difference exists—
and if you can't find a previously overlooked difference to explain away the
doubt—then the possible cause should be given the death sentence.

The Example

Off-Color Product Problem Matrix No. 5 (Figure 8.16) shows how the
Alloys, Inc., problem analysts took their possible cause (argon pressure)
through the testing phase, applying the testing question to each Is–Is Not
pair. As you can see, there's no way the argon pressure could cause the off-
color product because the defect—the off-color—was detected before
Alloy 123 ever got to the argon chamber.

The only possible cause that could be developed has been shot down.
There's no way that any change in the argon pressure could have caused the
problem. So where does this leave the team? For starters, there weren't any
doubts about the information contained in the Is and Is Not columns—
everything there was a fact that could be verified. Did the team members
overlook or miss one or more differences? Try as they might, the team
members couldn't come up with any. They then went back to the differences column, put each entry under a magnifying glass, and compiled this
information.

- *Hydrogen treatment.* The process hasn't been changed since the day
  we started it up; since the problem started we've virtually rebuilt
  the system and changed the hydrogen tanks.
- *Pulverizing method.* We haven't changed the equipment or the pro-
  cedure since the day we began making Alloy 123.
- *Eutectic alloy.* We're buying the same material from the same ven-
  dor we've used since the start and it meets all our incoming specs.
- *Blender.* We haven't changed anything and we stopped using it on
  October 5.
- *Argon chamber.* Nothing's been changed other than the new pres-
  sure regulator.
- *Operators.* They've all been on line 7 for years and they all do an
  excellent job of following our written procedures.
- *Location.* Line 7 has been where it is for years.

This is the point at which the nervous, undisciplined problem solver will
start to invent changes that never happened. The confident, disciplined
problem solver will step back, look at the problem dimension, and ask,
"What am I missing, what am I overlooking, what do I know about the
cause?"

DEVIATION STATEMENT: Off-color product

	IS	IS NOT	DIFFERENCES	CHANGES (TIMING)	TEST
WHAT					
Defect	Off-color product	Poor physical properties			?, argon is inert, doubt it could be cause but can't say no
Object	Alloy 123	Any other product	Hydrogen treatment		?, doubtful but can't say no as Alloy 123 chemistry differs
	Lot 81	Lots 80–01	Pulverizing method		OK, regulator changed between lots
WHERE					
Observed	Line 7	Other lines	Eutetic alloy raw material		OK, argon used only on line 7
			Hydrogen treatment		
			Pulverizers		
			Blender		
			Argon chamber	New pressure regulator (Aug. 12)	
			Operators		No, off-color seen before argon chamber
	After hydrogen treatment	Before	Location		
On object	Particle surface	Uniformly through particle			
	Entire surface	Part of surface			
WHEN					
Observed	Aug. 14	Aug. 11 or before			
On object	After hydrogen treatment	Before			
EXTENT					
How bad	Dark blue to black	Light green, other colors			
How many	Approx. 40% of lots	Standard = 0%, over 40%			
	25% to 100% of a lot	Less than 25%			
POSSIBLE CAUSE HYPOTHESIS	Greater or lesser argon pressure is affecting the color of Alloy 123.				

Figure 8.16   Off-Color Product Problem Matrix No. 5

Thinking logically about the Develop Possible Causes information, the team members decided that they might be overlooking some change. Thinking logically about the differences—the source of change—they recognized that two differences—the hydrogen and the eutectic alloy—came from external sources. (The argon also comes from an external source, but that had already been ruled out.) Was it possible that one or both of these vendors had changed what they were providing to the company? Could one or both have made a change in their manufacturing process that had altered, without their knowledge, the composition of what they were supplying?

As thinking problem solvers, the team members could only answer "Yes" to these possibilities. After answering yes, their next step was to *assume* (don't forget that big question mark!) that each of these components had been changed. This left them with Off-Color Product Problem Matrix No. 6 (Figure 8.17).

Their next step was to hypothesize a Possible Cause Statement for each of these hypothetical changes:

> Somewhere around the beginning of August, the composition of the hydrogen we use changed (contaminants, purity, etc.) in a way that affects the color of Alloy 123.

> Somewhere around the beginning of August, the composition of the eutectic alloy we use changed (contaminants, purity, etc.) in a way that affects the color of Alloy 123.

Now they had two *hypothetical* possible causes to be tested to determine which, if either, had any validity.

Off-Color Product Problem Matrix No. 7 (Figure 8.18) shows the result of testing the hydrogen possible cause against each Is–Is Not pair. As you can see, it was shot down by the "lot 81 versus lots 80-1" information because the hydrogen tanks were not changed at the time the color changed.

The problem analysts the moved on to the next possible cause and tested it. Off-Color Product Problem Matrix No. 8 (Figure 8.19) shows how the eutectic alloy possible cause fared against each Is–Is Not pair. A question about the cause was raised by the Alloy 123 versus any other product information. However, looking at this Is–Is Not pair shows that there is a difference between Alloy 123 and the other products: only Alloy 123 is subjected to the hydrogen treatment.

Therefore the Possible Cause Statement was recast to reflect a change plus difference possible cause:

DEVIATION STATEMENT: Off-color product

	IS	IS NOT	DIFFERENCES	CHANGES (TIMING)
WHAT				
Defect	Off-color product	Poor physical properties		
Object	Alloy 123	Any other product	Hydrogen treatment	Composition has changed? (around beginning of Aug.)
	Lot 81	Lots 80–01	Pulverizing method	
WHERE				
Observed	Line 7	Other lines	Eutetic alloy raw material	Composition has changed? (around beginning of Aug.)
			Hydrogen treatment	
			Pulverizers	
			Blender	
			Argon chamber	New pressure regulator (Aug. 12)
			Operators	
	After hydrogen treatment	Before	Location	
On object	Particle surface	Uniformly through particle		
	Entire surface	Part of surface		
WHEN				
Observed	Aug. 14	Aug. 11 or before		
On object	After hydrogen treatment	Before		
EXTENT				
How bad	Dark blue to black	Light green, other colors		
How many	Approx. 40% of lots	Standard = 0%, over 40%		
	25% to 100% of a lot	Less than 25%		

Figure 8.17   Off-Color Product Problem Matrix No. 6

DEVIATION STATEMENT: Off-color product				
	IS	IS NOT	DIFFERENCES	CHANGES (TIMING)	TEST

	IS	IS NOT	DIFFERENCES	CHANGES (TIMING)	TEST
WHAT					
Defect	Off-color product	Poor physical properties			
Object	Alloy 123	Any other product	Hydrogen treatment	Composition has changed? (around beginning of Aug.)	OK, hydrogen is known to affect the color OK, hydrogen used only for Alloy 123
	Lot 81	Lots 80–01	Pulverizing method		NO, hydrogen tanks last for over 50 lots, they were changed at lot 51 and then not until lot 99
WHERE					
Observed	Line 7	Other lines	Eutetic alloy raw material Hydrogen treatment Pulverizers Blender Argon chamber Operators Location	Composition has changed? (around beginning of Aug.) New pressure regulator (Aug. 12)	
	After hydrogen treatment	Before			
On object	Particle surface Entire surface	Uniformly through particle Part of surface			
WHEN					
Observed	Aug. 14	Aug. 11 or before			
On object	After hydrogen treatment	Before			
EXTENT					
How bad	Dark blue to black	Light green, other colors			
How many	Approx. 40% of lots 25% to 100% of a lot	Standard = 0%, over 40% Less than 25%			
POSSIBLE CAUSE HYPOTHESIS	Somewhere around the beginning of August, the composition of the hydrogen we use changed (contaminants, purity, etc.) in a way that affects the color of Alloy 123.				

Figure 8.18   Off-Color Product Problem Matrix No. 7

DEVIATION STATEMENT: Off-color product

	IS	IS NOT	DIFFERENCES	CHANGES (TIMING)	TEST
WHAT					
Defect	Off-color product	Poor physical properties			OK, color of eutectic is known to be affected by the process NO, why only Alloy 123 affected, eutectic is used in other alloys
Object	Alloy 123	Any other product	Hydrogen treatment	Composition has changed? (around beginning of Aug.)	
	Lot 81	Lots 80–01	Pulverizing method		
WHERE					
Observed	Line 7	Other lines	Eutectic alloy raw material Hydrogen treatment Pulverizers Blender Argon chamber Operators Location	Composition has changed? (around beginning of Aug.) New pressure regulator (Aug. 12)	
	After hydrogen treatment	Before	Before		
On object	Particle surface Entire surface	Uniformly through particle Part of surface			
WHEN					
Observed	Aug. 14	Aug. 11 or before			
On object	After hydrogen treatment	Before			
EXTENT					
How bad	Dark blue to black	Light green, other colors			
How many	Approx. 40% of lots 25% to 100% of a lot	Standard = 0%, over 40% Less than 25%			
POSSIBLE CAUSE HYPOTHESIS	Somewhere around the beginning of August, the composition of the eutectic alloy we use changed (contaminants, purity, etc.) in a way that affects the color of Alloy 123.				

Figure 8.19   Off-Color Product Problem Matrix No. 8

Somewhere around the beginning of August, the composition of the eutectic alloy we use changed (contaminants, purity, etc.) in a way that, when it is subjected to hydrogen treatment, affects the color of Alloy 123.

Off-Color Product Problem Matrix No. 9 (Figure 8.20) shows how this possible cause tested out. Three questions were raised about the possible cause (see the three ?? entries in the Test column of the matrix), which brought the problem analysts to the final step of the Problem Analysis process.

Step Five: Verify Most Probable Cause

The Test Possible Causes step involves validation of the Most Probable Cause against the problem specification, against the facts of the problem as defined by the Is and Is Not information. However, even if this testing has produced a perfect, undeniable match of the most probable cause to the problem specification, it is still prudent to now go out to the real world where the problem actually exists and verify in the actual problem environment that the most probable cause is indeed the true cause.

How do we do this? One obvious way is to undo the change embodied in the most probable cause and return the situation to the circumstances and parameters that existed before the problem started. If the problem goes away, that should be a good indication that you have indeed found the true cause.

However, in some instances it may not be possible to return to the pre-problem conditions. For example, the person who occupied the job before the problem started may have retired, the raw material you were using before the problem hit may no longer be available, or the company that used to perform the processing for you may have gone out of business. In situations like these, verification can be more difficult and there isn't any simple checklist of try this first, try this next, and so on. You are left to your own devices; think it out and do the best you can.

The Example

The team analyzing the off-color Alloy 123 had a most probable cause that, first, was based on an assumption (the composition of the eutectic alloy had changed) and, second, had three questions raised about it. The first question showed that the batch of eutectic alloy used for Alloy 123 lot 81 was different from the batch used for lot 80. Therefore, to find out whether the assumption was valid, the company would have to go to the manufac-

DEVIATION STATEMENT: Off-color product	IS	IS NOT	DIFFERENCES	CHANGES (TIMING)	TEST
WHAT					
Defect	Off-color product	Poor physical properties			OK, color of eutectic is known to be affected by the process
Object	Alloy 123	Any other product	Hydrogen treatment	Composition has changed? (around beginning of Aug.)	OK, eutectic only gets hydrogen treatment for Alloy 123
	Lot 81	Lots 80–01	Pulverizing method		?, possible, one batch of eutectic gives us five lots of Alloy 123, a new batch was used for lot 81
WHERE					
Observed	Line 7	Other lines	Eutectic alloy raw material	Composition has changed? (around beginning of Aug.)	OK, only line 7 uses both eutectic and hydrogen treatment
			Hydrogen treatment	New pressure regulator (Aug. 12)	
			Pulverizers		
			Blender		
			Argon chamber		
			Operators		
			Location		
On object	After hydrogen treatment	Before			OK, hydrogen treatment is known to affect color
	Particle surface	Uniformly through particle			OK, color only expected on the surface
	Entire surface	Part of surface			OK, entire surface is treated
WHEN					
Observed	Aug. 14	Aug. 11 or before			?, possible, line 7 gets new batch of eutectic every week
On object	After hydrogen treatment	Before			OK, hydrogen treatment is known to affect color
EXTENT					
How bad	Dark blue to black	Light green, other colors			OK, both eutectic and hydrogen affect color
How many	Approx. 40% of lots 25% to 100% of a lot	Standard = 0%, over 40% Less than 25%			?, possible, could be a marginal condition in the eutectic
POSSIBLE CAUSE HYPOTHESIS	Somewhere around the beginning of August, the composition of the eutectic alloy we use changed in a way that, when it is subjected to hydrogen treatment, affects the color of Alloy 123.				

Figure 8.20   Off-Color Product Problem Matrix No. 9

turer of the eutectic alloy and say that it suspected the manufacturer had changed something between these respective batches and see what the manufacturer had to say.

Essentially, this is what the company did. Once the team got to this point of the analysis late on a Friday afternoon after twenty hours of analysis, the vice president of manufacturing immediately called the vendor, reported that a crisis existed, and requested that the vendor's top technical and manufacturing people come to a meeting at the company's office the following Monday morning. At the meeting, the vice president walked the vendor's people through the entire Problem Analysis—which included revealing quite a bit of proprietary information—to show how the company had arrived at the conclusion that the eutectic alloy was the most likely culprit.

The meeting lasted two hours and the vendor's people left the company's office and started the four-hour trip back to their plant. Two hours later, the vice president got a phone call from the vendor's people. They had stopped at a roadside phone to call and let him know that—while discussing the problem as they drove—they had identified what they had thought at the time would be a minor, insignificant change in their manufacturing process that they had made near the end of July. At that time, no one had thought that the change would in any way affect the properties of their eutectic alloy. They said they were going to undo the change the first thing Tuesday morning and would deliver the first batch of the new "old" material the following week. Alloys, Inc., was back in business with Alloy 123 the following week.

By the way, for your amusement and/or enlightenment, you might be interested to know that several engineers on the Problem Analysis team had vociferously objected to approaching the vendor in the way that the vice president did. Their reasoning was that Alloys, Inc., was an insignificant customer for the vendor, who was the only source of this type of eutectic alloy and in a sold-out position and just might tell the company to take its business elsewhere, and finally that the possible cause was a stupid assumption to make because the eutectic alloy continued to conform to all the company's specifications.

Talk about failing to apply logical thought processes. What are material specifications other than an *assumed* set of measures that the purchaser *thinks* will define all its needs. Obviously, the company's specs for the eutectic alloy didn't define all those needs. Fortunately, the vice president of manufacturing was intelligent enough to recognize this possibility and proceed accordingly.

Before closing the book on this example, let's revisit the original problem specification to emphasize some ways of making the Problem Analysis process effective. Recall that this problem was initially simplified by ignoring everything that happened after lot 81, after August 14. Why? First, there was a sharp demarcation line between lots 80 and 81 that obviously offered a hot place to look for differences, for changes, for possible causes. Whether or not the other Is–Is Not lot numbers and dates would be a source of differences would remain to be seen. At minimum they might not reveal anything; at maximum they could bring out differences that would add a mound of trivia, potentially irrelevant information and needless complexity to the analysis. Moreover this information could have been contaminated by the thirteen changes they made along the way.

Once the most probable cause of a simplified problem has been verified, it obviously might be prudent to go back to the full specification to see if the same cause can account for each of the subsequent Is–Is Not lot numbers. This example did not show that step because in this case it wasn't necessary; the initial verification covered all the bases and demonstrated that a supposedly insignificant vendor's change in the eutectic alloy created a marginal, "shade of gray" situation in the company's process—sometimes the manufacturing process could accommodate the change and sometimes it couldn't.

You were told at the start that this wasn't going to be a simple, neat, or straightforward example. You were also told it would be a realistic example of the kind of situation that problem solvers can expect to find in the real world. What you weren't told was that, of the many Problem Analyses I've encountered over a twenty-year span, this was one of the simplest. Clearly, Problem Analysis requires a commitment of time and effort but, if you believe in the fundamental applied logic of the thinking process, it will show you the way—if you just play the game by the rules.

Some Closing Thoughts About Problem Solving

One Problem—One Cause

Many would-be problem solvers can't accept the fact that a given problem can have only *one cause*. Although that cause may have a couple of components, a change plus a difference for example (in twenty years of Problem Analysis projects, only once did I encounter a problem whose cause consisted of a change plus *two* differences), the combination of them constitutes one cause. If either component was missing, if the interaction wasn't there, the problem wouldn't have occurred.

If you come up with two or more possible causes that test out 100% and completely satisfy *every* Is–Is Not information pair, that's a red flag that something's wrong.

There are two likely explanations for this result. First, your specification may have actually lumped together two—or more—separate, discrete problems. In other words, you did an incomplete job of separating back in the Situation Assessment process or in constructing the Deviation Statement. The second possibility is that some of your Is–Is Not information is fantasy, not fact. In most cases where two or more possible causes satisfy all the parameters of the problem, it's because two or more separate problems have been combined—into a mess. This is most prevalent in the more subjective area of people problems.

A classic example of such a mess is the old catchall commonly referred to as a "morale problem" (which usually means a dozen different things to a dozen different people). The skilled problem solver will immediately separate this out, often to find a plethora of singular deviations such as unacceptable level of complaints about the cafeteria food, excessive turnover in the drafting department, lost-time accidents on the increase, and so on.

So what if a person does lump two problems, together, what's the big deal? The big deal is that the odds are the would-be problem solver will never find the true causes of the individual problems, thus they will likely persist. Also, most Problem Analysis subsequently leads to Decision Analysis; once cause is found, corrective action must be taken to get rid of the cause. If one composite corrective action is undertaken to try to get rid of two or more combined problems, the odds are great that the cost, complexity, and the like of that action will be much greater than if a separate, targeted, corrective action had been taken against each problem.

The fact that a single problem, a single deviation—as defined and discussed here—*cannot* have multiple causes is something that many would-be problem solvers can't—or won't—accept. One frequent reason for this is that the concept of multiple causes is a security blanket for many people; it's a way of keeping the buck in circulation, of stopping it from landing on their desks. It's a way of trying to close the book on getting out from beneath a problem that's been around too long or has cost too much. "The 'fact' that this problem has such a huge, complex, multifaceted cause explains why it took us so long to solve it (and why I'm not at fault)." Sometimes, as mentioned earlier, people will resist separating problems for the same reasons; they don't want to get to the one problem–one cause stage of analysis. For those who comprehend the logic system of Problem Analysis, it's obvious why a single problem can have only one cause.

I can't count the number of times I've been told about problems, supposedly *identical* problems, that seem to reappear every couple of weeks or months or years. If they truly are identical, this says that either the true cause wasn't found the first time around or that the action taken didn't correct the problem. Unfortunately, such recurrences are seldom seen as an indication of poor problem solving.

One other side excursion relative to cause needs to be dealt with. Sometimes when people have difficulty finding cause, they jump into making all kinds of changes in the situation in an attempt to *reproduce* the problem. If they succeed, they assume they've found the cause; the reality often is that they have succeeded in replicating the problem's *effect*, not in finding its *cause*.

The Problem Analysis process is a powerful tool that can be tremendously helpful if you don't forget its rules, if the problem solver doesn't try to take poetic license with the *facts* relating to the problem.

Fishbone Diagrams

Fishbone, or Ishikawa, or cause-and-effect diagrams are often touted as a valuable tool for finding the cause of a problem. In reality, they can be dangerous in that they can obscure cause. Why? Because once one constructs a fishbone diagram of a process, there's a natural tendency to assume that it's *all*-inclusive, that nothing has been overlooked, that everything that can affect the outcome has been depicted in the diagram. Just like the word "never," "everything" can be a dangerous word. If the problem solvers believe that they have identified all possible cause-and-effect relationships in the diagram, then one of the things they have identified will be named as the cause, no matter how much illogical thinking might be required to make it fit the facts. If the cause *has* to be on the fishbone, then it *will* be found there.

As an example, Figure 8.21 is a process classification type of diagram— constructed after the fact—based on the off-color product example. It includes what was learned about the avenues the company's people had explored and the actions they had taken in the three months before the Problem Analysis was done. Although they hadn't constructed a fishbone diagram of the process, Off-Color Product Fishbone No. 1 (Figure 8.21) illustrates what it probably would have looked like if they had taken that step. And if they had assumed it to contain the cause, they never would have solved the problem.

Off-Color Product Fishbone No. 2 (Figure 8.22) illustrates the additions that would have had to be made for the fishbone to be of assistance in locating cause. However, the company's people were initially blind to considering this next level of information because the eutectic alloy continued to conform to all the company's specifications. In effect, they had assumed not only that they knew all the possible causes but that the cause had to

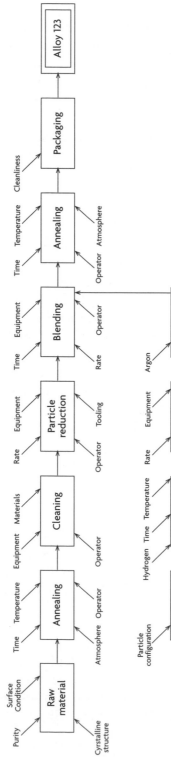

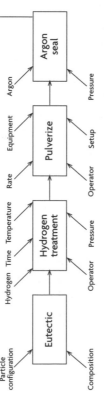

Figure 8.21 Off-Color Product Fishbone No. 1

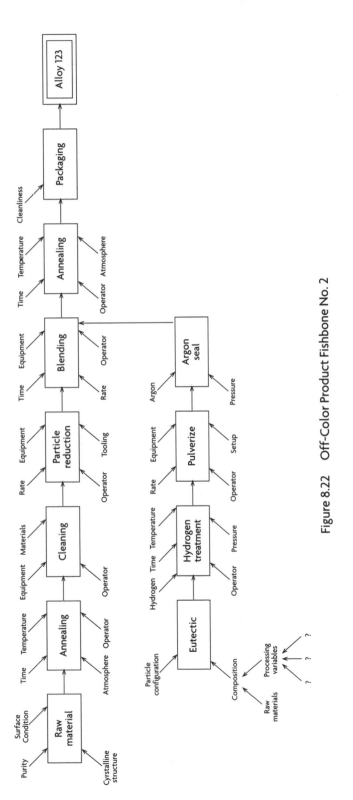

Figure 8.22 Off-Color Product Fishbone No. 2

lie within their four walls; they were in no position to draw a complete diagram.

Although fishbone diagrams can be seriously misleading in Problem Analysis, they can be useful in Potential Problem and Potential Opportunity Analysis. They can provide a path to identifying likely causes of potential problems or creating alternatives for potential opportunities.

Actions Related to Problem Analysis

Typically, completing a Problem Analysis—finding the cause—is not the end of the effort. The whole intent behind finding the cause is so that something can be done about it, and thus action is called for. In many Problem Analysis situations, once the cause is found, the best action to take is obvious—there isn't any need to undertake a formal Decision Analysis.

It is useful to recognize that there are three possible forms of action available relative to dealing with cause:

1. A Corrective Action, as the name implies, is one that removes a problem's cause. That's what was done in the off-color product problem; changing the eutectic alloy's manufacturing process back to what it had been eliminated the cause of the off-color product.
2. An Interim Action is a temporary action that may be taken before or after the cause is known. Its objective is to buy time, minimize the seriousness of the problem, or both. In the case of the off-color product, in the period before the cause was found the company eventually went on overtime to produce more of Alloy 123. Although this resulted in more bad product being produced, that was a small price to pay for enabling them to also get more good product to minimize the impact on their customers. (Remember the problem specification showed that about 40% of the lots experienced rejection; thus 60% were okay.)
3. An Adaptive Action is taken when it's not possible or practical to eliminate the cause. Suppose in the off-color product problem, for example, the manufacturer of the eutectic alloy had refused to change its manufacturing process back to its former state. In that case, the company making Alloy 123 would have had to adapt to the situation. They could have tried compensating for the marginal eutectic alloy by making changes in their process for Alloy 123; they could have offered the eutectic alloy manufacturer a premium price to make special batches for them; they could have offered

another manufacturer of eutectic alloys a lucrative contract to attempt to emulate the material they had purchased from their original vendor; and so on.

The World of Problem Analysis

You've just gone through an in-depth illustration of the application of the Problem Analysis tools to a manufacturing problem. But there's a wide world of Unplanned Past Change situations out there in which this thinking process can be used. For example:

- Find the cause of a sudden increase in employee turnover.
- Determine what was behind a dramatic increase in the sales of a particular product.
- Determine the cause of a serious accident in the plant.
- Find the cause of the premature failure of a particular component in a product.
- Determine why some new machines aren't performing up to their specifications.
- Find the cause of a minute defect in a product that only shows up after the customer receives it.
- Determine why some components are failing shortly after customers install them.
- Find the cause of a sudden decline in market share.

In Summary: Problem Analysis

The major concept steps of Problem Analysis are:

1. Define the Deviation Statement
   • Should – Actual = Deviation

2. Specify the Problem
   • *What defect* is present; what defects are not present?
   What object (item, person, etc.) is experiencing the defect; what objects are not?
   • *Where* is the defect *observed* (geographic or other location); where is it not observed?
   Where is the defect *on the object*; where on the object is the defect not present?
   • *When* is the defect *observed* (clock or calendar time); when is it not observed?

When does the defect appear *on the object* (when in its life cycle); when does it not appear?

- What is the *extent* of the problem; what is it not (*how many* objects are/are not involved)?

What is the *extent* of the individual defect; and what is it not (*how bad* is it?*)

3. Develop Possible Causes
   - Identify sharp-contrast Is–Is Not pairs
   - In what way(s) is the (Is) different from the (Is Not)?
   - What, if anything, has changed in this difference (and when did it change)?
   - How could this change (or change plus difference) cause the problem?

4. Test Possible Causes
   - If (possible cause) is the cause, how does it explain why the problem is (Is) and not (Is Not)?

5. Verify Most Probable Cause
   - How can I verify that this is the true cause?

Part III

THE ADVANCED TOOLBOX

Part II discussed and illustrated the fundamental concepts of Decision Analysis, Potential Problem Analysis, and Problem Analysis. Because these concepts are often used in problem-solving meetings, this section begins with a discussion of effective meetings in Chapter 9.

Chapter 10 offers some ways of adapting the Decision Analysis tools to special types of situations.

Chapter 11 explores the macro application of both Potential Problem Analysis and Potential Opportunity Analysis in larger, less targeted perspectives than were discussed earlier.

Finally, Chapter 12 focuses on creativity in problem solving, offering insights in this area for the serious problem solver who wants to encourage creativity while benefiting from the effectiveness of logical problem solving.

9

On the Role of Meetings

In today's world of increasingly rapid and broad change, seldom if ever does one person possess all the information required to "solve a problem." Thus meetings are increasingly relied on to bring together individuals who are supposedly relevant knowledge sources to solve a problem. A problem-solving meeting is, by definition, one in which a composite body of knowledge must be assembled to come to a conclusion otherwise not possible because all those who possess this knowledge would not come together in the normal course of events.

Quite often the concepts described in this book will be helpful in problem-solving meetings. By itself, the use of the concepts doesn't guarantee a flawless meeting. To achieve an optimum solution via such a meeting requires that many factors be considered in arranging and conducting the meeting. The objective of this chapter is to identify and discuss those factors. For the purpose of simplicity, these meetings will collectively be referred to as problem-solving meetings.

The concerns that must be tackled via problem-solving meetings are the ones that amount to big round pegs when the organization structure consists of small square holes. They overlap conventional boundaries and their outcome has effects beyond the neat little square holes.

A Perspective

You have probably been a participant in many problem-solving meetings in which everyone had only one fond wish: "Let's get this waste of time over with." Why? The literature is replete with thoughts on the subject:

> Even at some of the best-run companies, they can't manage meetings. No one teaches them how.[1]

> It's likely that no other business event is as misunderstood, poorly planned, and poorly conducted as the small meeting.[2]

> The meeting remains the most fundamental decision making system in ... our society. ... However, the *process* [emphasis added] by which such decisions are made is often ambiguous and unproductive, the result of which is less than quality decisions.[3]

> If a meeting is unsuccessful, the fault is squarely that of the person running the meeting.[4]

Problem-solving meetings are the most difficult type of meeting to conduct. Such a meeting lives or dies on interaction and information flow. Many participants walk into these meetings certain that they already know exactly what information is going to be needed to solve the problem. Seldom, if ever, do their prescriptions for success prove completely accurate. The successful resolution of most issues ultimately depends on uncovering at least a few pieces of previously unrecognized information. And more often than not, the key to uncovering these hidden gems lies in the thinking-process skills of the meeting leader.

The Agenda

The gospel according to many meeting "experts" is that you should *always* provide a detailed agenda for *every* meeting. I disagree strongly! For a problem-solving meeting, *never* provide more than a simple statement of the issue to be dealt with and a guesstimate of how long the process will take. The simple reason is that—unless you're stacking the deck toward a predetermined conclusion—it is not possible to accurately predict how long each step will take. So keep your options open and don't give the participants a reason to wonder why the meeting is ahead of or behind schedule or why the leader added or skipped a step.

Leader versus Facilitator

The label of "facilitator" has become a vogue term to apply to people who are supposedly skilled in leading problem-solving meetings. What is a facilitator? What does a facilitator do, how does he or she operate? Many academic definitions suggest that a facilitator's role is to operate in a reactive mode and lead a meeting *only* when the group wants him or her to perform that role; in other words, there may be occasions when the group wants to control the meeting. I advocate what is known as the Participative-Process Consulting (PPC) mode. The three elements of PPC are:

1. The participative-process consultant's role is to help the group come up with an optimum solution for the situation it must resolve.
2. The consultant leads the group through a process that the consultant controls; the group controls the content.
3. The consultant operates in a *proactive* mode and controls the direction and progress of the group.

Some elements of the facilitator's role are contrary to this. Therefore, I've chosen to use the term "leader" instead of facilitator.

The Meeting Leader

In a problem-solving meeting, the leader need not be knowledgeable about the *content information*, the facts that define the problem or the particulars that are relevant to the decision or potential problem to be dealt with. A lack of content knowledge can actually be an important contributing factor to a meeting leader's objectivity toward the participants' content knowledge.

Regardless of the type of problem, the key to effectively resolving it lies in the meeting leader's skill in applying the appropriate thinking process(es)—the appropriate thoughtware—to the discussion and in his or her distance from the problem.

Distance is extremely important to leader effectiveness. The role of a meeting leader and the role of a meeting participant are mutually exclusive. The same person *cannot* play both roles effectively; they are contradictory and they conflict. If a problem-solving meeting is to accomplish its desired result quickly and effectively, the person leading the meeting should *not* be a contributor of content information about the problem.

The meeting leader is there because he or she knows how to process, how to analyze, and how to assemble the pieces of the content information to arrive at a solution. If the meeting leader starts to inject content knowledge into the meeting, he or she immediately becomes suspect in the participants' eyes ("Aha, the leader is trying to steer us toward a predetermined answer"). From that point on, the leader's credibility with the group will wane. To be effective, the meeting leader should possess *stranger value*, which is what distance is all about.

Some readers may have difficulty accepting the two preceding paragraphs. I strongly believe what they state, yet I'm willing to consider a few "ifs": *if* a leader-participant is felt by all the other participants to truly be interested in the best answer and not have any bias toward the outcome; *if* the leader-participant only injects content information that was overlooked by everyone else after they all had their say, and *if* the other participants see this new information as valid, not as an attempt to stack the deck; *if* the leader-participant readily backs off when contradicted by another participant, then, maybe, a leader-participant can be effective. But those are a lot of ifs.

A meeting called to solve a problem can be run effectively by someone from within the organization *if* that person is perceived by the participants as being distant from the problem. That is, in the participants' eyes the leader won't be affected by the outcome—he or she could not care less about the ultimate solution as long as it was reached through an effective process.

In addition to distance, the leader must possess two other critical elements. First, the participants must see the leader as a person with sufficient stature to run the meeting. If the participants are all seasoned vice presidents, it's highly unlikely that they will open up to a leader twenty years younger who has just been hired by the Training Department. Regardless of this person's skills, he or she will usually be faced with losing an uphill battle.

The second critical element follows from the first and is related to the sensitivity of the problem to be resolved. Even when the leader is of an age that is acceptable to the participants and is well qualified, if he or she is newly hired and the issue is sensitive, the chances are slim that the participants will be willing to openly discuss it in this person's presence.

In an effective problem-solving meeting, the leader is the meeting CEO and the participants—regardless of their jobs or titles—are peers of each other. The effective meeting leader must have the backbone to tell any and every participant that he or she is off base if and when this is necessary. (Ideally, this should never be necessary—unfortunately, sometimes it is.)

If an inside meeting leader isn't available who meets all these criteria—distance, stature, a right to hear sensitive information, and an ability to confront—the organization will have to go outside for a leader if it wants an effective resolution.

While on the subject of an internal versus external leader, there's one other element to examine. Often organizations, and the people who populate them, build up defenses over the years against doing things—such as solving problems—any way but our way or my way. Personal defenses are usually easy to spot and deal with. However, an internal meeting leader may be oblivious to organizational defenses because they have become a subconscious, integral part of his or her modus operandi. Such defenses have the potential to impact an internal leader's effectiveness.

To sum up, there are several important factors to consider in selecting a person to lead a problem-solving team:

- The leader should be exceptionally skilled in using the thinking process(es) that the analysis will require.
- The leader should *not* be exceptionally knowledgeable about the issue to be resolved.
- The leader should *not* have a vested interest in any particular outcome for the analysis.
- The leader should be a person who will be accepted by the group, *not* one whose presence or role could intimidate any of the participants, as well as a person who can confront any participant.

The Participants

The meeting participants should be there because they possess content knowledge about the problem. If a meeting is called to decide where to put a new office to serve your customers better, those chosen to participate in the meeting should possess knowledge of where these customers are located, what functions could best be handled in a regional office, and any other relevant issues.

There are several guidelines to consider when selecting team members:

- Select people who are closest to the situation, who have direct, hands-on knowledge about it, who understand its importance and will be responsible for making the results happen.
- Select only the people necessary to bring together the composite body of knowledge likely to be required; don't duplicate this

knowledge with extra people. Ideally a team should have no more than eight people on it.

- One of Parkinson's Laws—that he forgot to write—goes something like: "The complexity of accomplishing something with a group increases as the square (the cube?) of the number of people involved." If it takes a dozen people to bring together the necessary body of knowledge, so be it; but be prepared to pay the price: a significant slowdown in the speed of the analysis.
- In some situations, a team can be too small. If the situation requires only three or four people, and if they don't know each other, they may hesitate to open up. If this could be the case, it might be desirable to salt the meeting with a couple of people who are not needed for content but can help the discussion progress more smoothly. These people should be links or bridges between the needed team members; they should be known by these other team members.
- In some situations, particularly where creative insight could be critical, it may be desirable to have one or two "wild cards" on the team—people who know little or nothing about the issue at hand but have the potential to enlarge the group's perspective.
- An "observer" sitting in on a problem-solving meeting is a no-no. Regardless of the explanation offered to the group for the observer's presence, the odds are high that this presence will negatively affect the participation of some team members who may feel they are being "spied on."
- Select people who are open, independent thinkers, not introverts, yes persons, or egotists.
- Make sure that all the constituencies that could be affected by the outcome of the analysis or involved in making the results happen are represented on the team.
- Everyone on the team should *want* to be there; no one should be there because "my boss told me to come." The team members should "mesh well" with each other; people with clashing personalities should be avoided along with people likely to have hidden agendas.
- The makeup of the team should be such that it can proceed to implement the problem solution or the decision reached; a team that has to submit a recommendation for someone else to accept— or reject—has had the wrong composition from the start. Anyone who could say "No" to the outcome should be on the team.

As you proceed, if it becomes evident that a key knowledge area isn't represented, you can always make a phone call and ask someone with that knowledge to join the team or perhaps sit in for an hour or so at the appropriate stage of the process. You can always add people to a team, but be aware that it can be difficult to remove them.

Sometimes it might be best to use two or more teams in an analysis. In a Decision Analysis relative to a company's financial practices, for example, the objectives to be met by the outcome are probably best articulated by top management. However, they may be ill equipped to determine how best to accomplish them. In such a situation, you might use a top management team to establish and value the objectives and then send them home and bring in a new team of accounting and financial people to create and select the best alternative(s) based on the first team's objectives.

In a Potential Problem Analysis concerned with eliminating problems that could occur when a new facility is started up (e.g. a new bakery), it might be appropriate to use one team to look at the ingredients-handling area, another team for the mixing operations, another one for the baking area, and yet another for the packaging operations. Recognize, however, that in such multiple-team situations it usually makes sense to have a few people who are on all the teams to provide continuity and linkage across all the analyses.

Conducting the Meeting

People

In many problem-solving meetings, the participants walk in with more than their content knowledge; many of them have already made up their minds as to how the problem should be solved. This is known as the "don't confuse me with the facts" syndrome. There are a multitude of behaviors that participants can bring to a meeting that range from supportive to destructive. There is one simple rule for the meeting leader as far as dealing with disruptive participants: stick to the process—control it, don't hesitate to let participants know when their inputs aren't relevant to the process step being pursued at the moment, and keep a lively pace.

Time and Place

The most effective way of conducting a problem-solving meeting is to do it in one shot; determine how many days you think the analysis will require and ask the participants to plan their schedules accordingly. A few hours here and a few hours there, with days or weeks in between, typically leads to mediocre results. Why? There are many reasons, including these: Participants' recollections of what was accomplished in the preceding meeting often fade or shift, thus considerable time can be wasted in bringing everyone back up to speed. Often not every participant is present for every meeting, thus the inputs and perspectives can vary from meeting to meeting. In the interim, some participants may attempt to influence other participants to alter their positions. The status of what's going on, what's being discussed, can inadvertently or intentionally be "leaked" to those who might exert pressure to change things. Outsiders who think they know what's going on, what's being discussed, or where people are coming from, can start rumors that can put the participants in difficult positions when they are asked to corroborate them. Stick with the job until it is done.

One exception to this guideline is the situation in which the team doesn't initially possess all the information required to carry the analysis through to its conclusion. In this circumstance, start the analysis and go as far as the available information permits. At this point, you'll know exactly what information is missing. Then make specific information-gathering assignments and adjourn. Reconvene the meeting at a predetermined date to complete the analysis.

Problem-solving meetings should not be burn-the-midnight-oil meetings. This type of meeting is mentally demanding and draining. After seven or eight hours, fatigue starts to take its toll and people's thinking gets sloppy; sloppy thinking is a guaranteed prescription for mediocre results.

There's a school of thought that says that when lunch time arrives, adjourn for an hour and let the participants go their own way and do their own thing. I don't subscribe to that philosophy; when I conduct problem-solving meetings, I insist that lunch be brought into the meeting room and that we get started again in a half hour. It's been my experience that this keeps people energized and focused; most important, it keeps the mood from being broken.

The meeting should be held in a place where the participants won't be subject to interruptions for phone calls or other demands. The location should be one in which you don't have to worry about the sensitivity of the issue being discussed. Don't use a location where some of the participants in a controversial situation might feel that they have a "home court advantage."

The meeting room itself should be appropriate for the size of the team, not too big or too small—people should have room to move around but not rattle around—and it must have all the necessary audiovisual and other support equipment. Above all, it should have classroom-level lighting.

Visibility

It's impossible to organize and apply the concepts—and the information they bring forth—"in your head." In each process, there's a specific format at work that organizes the information being used for each successive step.

On the job, particularly when working in teams, there's no substitute for flip charts for making your analysis visible. When working on flip charts, everyone involved is focused on the same information. Flip charts enable you to use different colors to identify different types of information. Most important, flip charts can be saved for future revisits, reviews, and analysis reviews.

Summary

The success of a problem-solving meeting depends on the leader's competence and the right choice of team members, of those who will bring the relevant content knowledge to the analysis. Its success is a function of the leader's ability to utilize the appropriate thinking process(es) to control the participation and the information flow. A well-conducted problem-solving meeting can be a stimulating experience for everyone. No doubt you are well aware of the effect a poorly conducted meeting can have.

10

Specialized Decision Analysis Tools

Chapter 5 illustrated the fundamental tools of Decision Analysis (Figure 10.1). This chapter examines three special applications of the Decision Analysis concepts:

1. Priority Setting
2. The Phantom Alternative
3. The Day-One Deviation

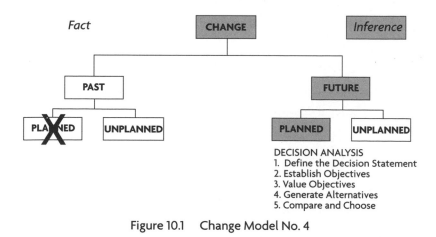

Figure 10.1   Change Model No. 4

Priority Setting

Back in Chapter 4 on Situation Assessment, it was mentioned that priority setting is nothing other than application of Decision Analysis, and that some priority-setting situations require a full-blown application of the Decision Analysis tools. One such priority-setting situation is the selection of product-development projects. Often there are more project ideas vying for attention and resources than an organization could ever begin to pursue. Furthermore, in such situations objectivity is often thin at best as each person pushes for his or her pet idea to be at the head of the list.

Here is how Decision Analysis was used in a priority-setting effort undertaken by a machinery manufacturer. The Decision Statement was:

Select the optimum development projects to pursue.

The objectives used, and their weighted values, were as follows:

10 Maximum operating income potential (three years after introduction).
10 Maximum return on dedicated assets.
10 Maximum support of expected future market direction(s).
9 Maximum revenue potential (three years after introduction).
9 Maximum potential increase in market shares (three years after introduction).
8 Good fit with expected business cycle conditions.
7 Provide effective opposition to expected competitive situation.
7 The technology that will be required is known and available.
6 We can provide significant competitive uniqueness.
5 It will fill a critical void in our product line.
4 Doesn't require long-term irrevocable financial commitment.
2 It can be accomplished with our existing skills.
87 (The sum of these weights—the reason for this follows.)

In addition, the team had one must objective:

M Any potential unique liability risk must be acceptable to our corporate legal department.

Regarding this must objective, the priority-setting team's intent was to send its final list of choices to the company's legal department, along with commentary on each product's expected application, and to indicate the dates on which the respective development work would start. It would then be up to the legal department to get back to the team with any concerns it had.

The team then created a scale of satisfaction for each objective. Remember that the top relative fit in any objective's scale of satisfaction is 10. Since the sum of the weights of the objectives was 87, and since a perfect alternative would receive a relative fit of 10 against each objective, a perfect alternative would have a total weighted score of 870.

The team evaluated eighteen alternatives (A through R) in carrying out a standard Decision Analysis. Since a perfect alternative would have a total weighted score of 870, an alternative coming in at the 75th percentile would have a total weighted score of 653 (870 x .75 = 653), one coming in at the 50th percentile would have a total weighted score of 435 (870 x .5 = 435), and so on.

The team decided that regardless of an alternative's utilization of the resources available, any alternative that came in below the 50th percentile would be dropped from consideration because of its inadequacy in satisfying their objectives. As a result, they ended up with seven projects to potentially pursue.

	Alternative	Total Weighted Score
1.	G	688
2.	N	579
3.	L	567
4.	R	565
5.	C	554
6.	I	510
7.	P	462

What did the team members have in this list of seven alternatives? All they had was an array of the relative attractiveness of those projects whose total weighted score was above the 50th percentile. To turn this initial list into a final list of projects to be pursued, they had to ascertain each project's estimated resource demands and determine the cumulative demand of the projects accrued sequentially through the list.

Because the company was under a corporate hiring freeze, staff availability was a limiting resource. The team members determined that they had five engineers who could be assigned to the new projects as well as four technicians and four draftsmen. As far as nonsalary dollars were concerned, they had $800,000 available to them for the coming year. The Resource Matrix of Figure 10.2 shows how they put the pieces together.

When they got as far as Project C on the list, they had exceeded their availability of engineers and draftsmen by .25 persons in each case. However, they still had $50,000 of nonsalary dollars available and .25 of a technician. Although staffing and money would be tight and had to be

| PROJECT | Dollars Required | | Engineers Required | | Technicians Required | | Draftsmen Required | |
	Project	Cumulative	Project	Cumulative	Project	Cumulative	Project	Cumulative
Available		$800K		5		4		4
G	$190K	$190K	1	1	2	2	1.5	1.5
N	$140K	$330K	1	2	0.5	2.5	0.5	2
L	$200K	$530K	1.5	3.5	0.5	3	1	3
R	$180K	$710K	1.5	5	0.5	3.5	1	4
C	$40 K	$750K	0.25	5.25	0.25	3.75	0.25	4.25

Figure 10.2   Resource Matrix

managed very carefully, they felt they could contract out the engineering and drafting work on Project C and come through on target. Thus the team drew the line on next year's projects after Project C, dropping Projects I and P.

This use of the Decision Analysis process is effective in any situation where priorities are an issue.

The Phantom Alternative

Once you really get a feel for and an understanding of the Decision Analysis process, you'll become aware of opportunities to adjust it to accommodate special situations. One of the most useful manipulations is what is aptly described as the phantom alternative. Here's an example of how it works.

Suppose you're going to be on a several-weeks-long, college-recruiting trip. Specifically, you're looking to hire several new graduates for field sales positions. (Although you may intend to hire several, you're still in the select mode—the alternatives are mutually exclusive. If you have 10 positions available and expect to interview about 100 candidates, 90 of them won't be getting offers.) You define your Decision Statement as "Select the best field-sales candidates," and you do a thorough job of establishing and valuing the relevant objectives; you're all set to go.

But, wait a minute, it will be almost a month from the time you interview the first candidate until you interview the last one. Suppose your gut feel says that the first interviewee is a hot candidate. If you wait a month until you've had a chance to interview all the candidates to decide which ones you want to proceed further with, that first candidate might think he or she is low on your list because it took you so long to respond. The person might even have accepted another job offer in the interim. Besides, how can you expect to remember all your impressions about that first candidate a month later? You need a way to make quick, initial evaluation of each candidate.

Enter the concept of the phantom alternative. First, take each objective and think about what realistically would constitute the best satisfaction of it that you could reasonably expect to see. Use this as the 10 and create a satisfaction scale for that objective. Consider what would constitute total failure to meet the objective and thus define the 0, the bottom of the scale. Now define one or more levels of satisfaction between the 10 and the 0. Finally, do this for all the other objectives.

Objective: Excellent people skills (Weight = 10)	
Satisfaction Scale	*Score*
Acceptably outgoing, listens well, good eye contact, asks good questions	10
Some fixable weaknesses in the above	5
Introvert	0

Starting with the first objective, look at its scale and decide the point at which a minimally acceptable candidate would just make the cut. Considering the importance of "Excellent people skills," let's assume you feel a candidate should merit at least a relative fit of 7 on this scale to be considered; multiplying this times the objective's weight of 10 yields a weighted score of 70.

Do this for all the objectives, then multiply these relative fits times the weights of their corresponding objectives and add them up to get the total weighted score of the phantom alternative, a hypothetically satisfactory candidate. You now have a tool that you can use after every interview, or at the end of the day, to evaluate candidates. If a candidate's total weighted score doesn't come up to that of the phantom alternative's, you would drop that person from further consideration. On the other hand, if a candidate's total weighted score dramatically exceeded that of the phantom alternative—say, if it was at the 95th percentile—you might want to immediately activate the recruiting process for that person.

The college-recruiting trip example depicts the use of the phantom alternative concept for evaluating different alternatives over a period of time. This concept can also be helpful in situations where dozens, if not hundreds, of alternatives are parceled out among members of a committee who are to make an initial cut at deciding which alternatives should be dropped from further consideration.

The following example is taken from a university's presidential search committee. The committee of a dozen people constructed a list of thirty-one objectives to use in making their selection. Given the diversity of the group, and the fact that selecting a president was a first-time experience for everyone, the participants were uncomfortable using a 10 to 1 weighting system for the objectives; they felt that that range implied more precision and ability to minutely differentiate than they possessed. Therefore, they chose to use a 3 to 1 weighting scale.

The committee's Decision Statement was:

Select the best president for (our) university.

Following is the list of objectives the committee members developed and the weights they assigned to them:

3 Has excellent academic credentials and credibility.
3 Really enjoys working with people.
3 Is comfortable with being highly visible.
3 Has excellent fund-raising leadership abilities.
3 Has good ability to enhance image and reputation of university on and off campus as a preeminent educational institution.
3 Has good ability to recognize, communicate, and coordinate differing views of major constituencies.
3 Brings good, relevant, pragmatic, managerial experience.
3 Is very resilient, able to change with the times and move forward.
3 Is an honest, straightforward person; doesn't play games.
3 Is firmly committed to, and tolerant of, individual liberties.
3 Is willing to stand up to the Board when he/she feels it must be done.
3 Has excellent ability to inspire others.
3 Is an open, leading-edge thinker, willing to "go out of the box" to try new creative ideas, willing to take risks.
3 Shows a definite "where should we be going" leadership attitude through inclusive style.
3 Is a good, quick, on-the-job learner and can be respected for his/her intelligence.
3 Is very energetic.
3 Can gain and hold respect.
3 Is a thoughtful and yet decisive strategist—thinks about what he/she does against long-term purposes.
3 Has no chemical dependencies that impede job performance.
3 Has good personal health.

3 Has academic background and interests broadly related to and supportive of our university's curricula.

3 Shows an inclusive management style—gathers support and develops consensus.

3 Is an excellent public speaker.

2 Can readily and fully become a part of our university's tradition.

2 Has an acceptable interest in, appreciation for, and leadership of student athletic concepts.

2 Understands and is supportive of fraternities and sororities.

2 Shows a high degree of self-confidence.

2 Is not afraid to travel by air.

1 Has a good personal appearance.

1 Has no unacceptable criminal record.

1 Has an excellent sense of humor, can laugh at self.

It's been my experience that most people and groups, left to their own devices, will develop very superficial, shallow sets of objectives. In my mind, the preceding set is an excellent, comprehensive, well-thought-out list and worth showing in its entirety. However, although this is the list the committee developed, not all the objectives were used for its initial cut, for defining the phantom alternative. Why? The reason was that the initial cut, the drop or consider further determination, had to be made based on resumes and background information furnished to the committee about the candidates. Evaluating the candidates against the full range of the objectives would require additional information and observations obtained during face-to-face interviews or reference checks. Therefore, to make this first cut, the committee culled out four objectives to be used by its members against the list of over 100 candidates whose resumes and background information had been provided.

Yes, by eliminating many candidates based on just these four objectives, the committee ran the risk of eliminating the best candidate. The committee realized this, but wasn't concerned. They had to be realistic; a committee of a dozen busy trustees, faculty, alumni, and students from all over the country could, at best, manage to convene for a day every couple of weeks. They needed a quick, objective way of narrowing their focus to the cream of the crop. The phantom alternative approach met their needs. (See the Candidate Selection Form.)

The sum of the weights of these four objectives was 12; thus a "perfect" candidate would have received a total weighted score of 120 (12 x 10 = 120). The phantom alternative received a total weighted score of 85 (71st percentile) and that score became their drop or consider further cutoff point.

Candidate Selection Form

Candidate no. _____   Committee member _____

Objective	Weight		
Has excellent academic credentials and credibility.	3		

			Weight x
Satisfaction Scale	Scale	Score	Score
Terminal degree and has come up through the professional ranks.	10	_____	_____
Master's degree plus broad academic experience.	5	_____	_____
Bachelor's degree only with no academic experience.	0	_____	_____

Objective	Weight		
Has excellent fund-raising abilities.	3		

			Weight x
Satisfaction Scale	Scale	Score	Score
Has delivered proven results for organizations similar to ours more than once in the past.	10	_____	_____
Has had some successful involvement but has never been the quarterback.	5	_____	_____
Has never done it or has tried and failed.	0	_____	_____

Objective	Weight		
Brings good, relevant, pragmatic managerial experience.	3		

Satisfaction Scale	Scale	Score	Weight x Score
Excellent proven credentials and track record in similar type of organization.	10	___	___
Proven as a middle manager but has never been at the top.	5	___	___
No managerial experience or has failed as a manager.	0	___	___

Objective	Weight		
Has academic background and interests relative to and supportive of our curricula.	3		

Satisfaction Scale	Scale	Score	Weight x Score
Has background as teacher and scholar in medium-size academic culture embodying arts and sciences.	10	___	___
Has some medium-size academic background but not in an intense, broad, academic culture.	5	___	___
Has only big university or big business background.	0	___	___

Total Weighted Score	___

The Day-One Deviation

Chapter 8 discussed deviations (problems) that take the form shown in Figure 10.3. Many times, problem solvers have to deal with a situation that *seems* to be similar to this illustration, but actually should be depicted as shown in Figure 10.4.

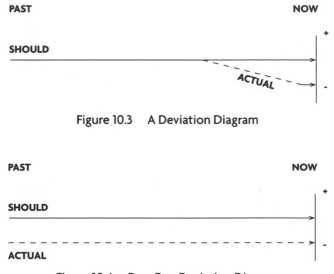

Figure 10.3   A Deviation Diagram

Figure 10.4   Day-One Deviation Diagram

The reason such a situation is often referred to as a day-one deviation is that the actual has deviated from the should since the process first began. Because of its similarity to a Problem Analysis situation, often the problem solvers' immediate reaction is to apply Problem Analysis tools to it. Stop. First of all, this isn't a true *deviation*. To deviate is "to *vary* from a uniform state." The actual in this case hasn't deviated or varied from the should because it's never been the same as the should. Recall the fundamental model of Past/Future, Planned/Unplanned Change. A Problem Analysis situation is one in which the problem solver is out to find the cause of an Unplanned Past Change. There isn't any such beast present here.

An Example

A manufacturer of specialized plastics used in the electrical industry was having difficulty keeping up with the times. A competitor had introduced a new product a year earlier with much higher insulation resistance than previously attainable. This characteristic was very desirable for certain applications; as a result, the company was shut out of those applications. Try as they might, after many months of effort they hadn't been able to produce a material that met this new standard.

The Thinking Process

What this situation calls for is Planned Future Change; it needs Decision Analysis. The problem solver must do something different in the future to attempt to move the actual to, or at least closer to, the should. (Whether this is possible will not be known until, if and when, it is actually achieved.)

Although a day-one deviation situation is clearly and unequivocally a Decision Analysis situation—there *is* a way in which part of the Problem Analysis thinking approach can be helpful in such situations. By definition, the reason that actual isn't meeting should is that an appropriate change hasn't been made or, in Decision Analysis terms, an appropriate alternative hasn't been applied to the situation. The key to success in this type of situation lies in the Generate Alternatives step of Decision Analysis, and part of the Problem Analysis thinking process can lend a hand in this step. Using what is known about the situation, construct an Is–Is Not worksheet (a problem specification matrix as described in Chapter 8) for the what and where dimensions of the situation. (The when and extent dimensions usually aren't helpful here.)

Back to the Example

Resorting to the day-one deviation concept, the problem-solving team drafted an Is–Is Not matrix (Plastics Company Possible Alternatives Matrix No. 1, shown in Figure 10.5).

Back to the Thinking Process

In most situations like this, the differences between the Is and the Is Not aren't known but, as a starting point, guesses can be made. Therefore, you need to add a *possible* differences column to the matrix. Also, in such situations the list of possible differences is often quite lengthy. Therefore, to help with eventually deciding "What do we check out first?" you also need to add a P column (for probability—high, medium, or low), in which guesses are made as to the probability of each possible difference actually existing.

DEVIATION STATEMENT: Determine the best way(s) to increase the insulation resistance of Product X		
	IS	IS NOT
WHAT Defect	Low insulation resistance	Poor dielectric strength, dimensional stability, thermal stability, etc.
Object	Our Product X	Competitor's Product X
WHERE Observed	All over	Localized
On object	Our lab	Elsewhere

Figure 10.5   Plastics Company Possible Alternatives Matrix No. 1

Back to the Example

The group working on this immediately zeroed in on "our Product X versus competitor's Product X" as the key, sharp-contrast information pair to dig into for possible differences. This led to Possible Alternatives Matrix No. 2 (Figure 10.6).

Back to the Thinking Process

In the Problem Analysis mode, the information in the differences column

DEVIATION STATEMENT: Determine the best way(s) to increase the insulation resistance of Product X				
	IS	IS NOT	POSSIBLE DIFFERENCES	P
WHAT Defect	Low insulation resistance	Poor dielectric strength, dimensional stability, thermal stability, etc.		
Object	Our Product X	Competitor's Product X	Polymer composition Additives composition Additives particle size Additives preparation Additives percentage Mixing conditions Extrusion conditions	L M H H H H M
WHERE Observed	All over	Localized		
On object	Our lab	Elsewhere		

Figure 10.6   Plastics Company Possible Alternatives Matrix No. 2

becomes a source of potential information about past change (cause). In the Decision Analysis mode, the information in the possible differences column becomes a source of ideas for possible changes (alternatives). Just as the list of possible differences can be lengthy, the list of possible changes can be even longer. Therefore, in addition to adding a possible changes column, you need to add another P (for probability) column to assess the likelihood of each possible change accomplishing the desired end result (Figure 10.7).

In some situations involving day-one deviations, you may use this tool and come up with a lengthy list of alternatives, with each one expensive and time consuming to try out. In such cases, you may choose to subject the alternatives you have generated to a Decision Analysis to put them in priority order.

Back to the Example

The team members then started to look at the high-probability possible differences entries to develop possible changes to generate alternatives that they could try. That resulted in the possible changes and their respective probabilities of success shown in Figure 10.7.

The outcome was that the team had the following high-probability possible changes ideas to try:

A. Decrease additives particle size by 25%.

B. Add moisture removal step and then inert gas atmosphere to the mixing operation.

The objective of this example is to illustrate the day-one deviation concept, not to get into the chemistry and physics of specialized plastics. Neither A nor B independently produced sufficient change in the product's insulation resistance. However, together they did move it in the right direction. The researchers then looked at a medium-probability possible change:

C. Increase additives percentage by 5%.

A combination of A, B, and C (with C finally at 8%) got them to their desired destination.

The Thinking Process

To sum things up, the Problem Analysis process can be adapted to finding ways of dealing with day-one deviations by using the Possible Alternatives Matrix shown in Figure 10.8.

	IS	IS NOT	POSSIBLE DIFFERENCES	P	POSSIBLE CHANGES	P
DEVIATION STATEMENT: Determine the best way(s) to increase the insulation resistance of Product X						
WHAT Defect	Low insulation resistance	Poor dielectric strength, dimensional stability, thermal stability, etc.				
Object	Our Product X	Competitor's Product X	Polymer composition	L		
			Additives composition	M		
			Additives particle size	H	Increase by 25%	L
					Decrease by 25%	H
			Additives preparation	H	Use halogenated solvent	L
			Additives percentage	H	Increase by 5%	M
					Decrease by 5%	L
			Mixing conditions	H	Add moisture removal step and then inert gas	H
			Extrusion conditions	M		
WHERE Observed	All over	Localized				
On object	Our lab	Elsewhere				

Figure 10.7   Plastics Company Possible Alternatives Matrix No. 3

	IS	IS NOT	POSSIBLE DIFFERENCES	P	POSSIBLE CHANGES	P
WHAT						
WHERE						

Figure 10.8   Possible Alternatives Matrix

Other Decision Analysis Tools

There are a multitude of other processes beyond these three special applications for thinking out decision situations and making choices, and a few broad comments about the genre may be useful. These other tools include Bayes Theorem, Decision Trees, Force Field Analysis, Game Theory, Histograms, Linear Programming, Monte Carlo Simulation, Multivariate Attribute Analysis, Probability Theory, Sensitivity Analysis, Trade-Off Analysis, and Utility Theory.

Many of these, such as Game Theory, Linear Programming, and Monte Carlo Simulation, can be useful in narrow, specialized applications. Some, such as Decision Trees, Force Field Analysis, and Trade-Off Analysis, can be dangerous and deceptive in that they *start out* by focusing on alternatives and their possible consequences and outcomes. Thus the decision makers can be deprived of the value of first thinking out *all* of the desired objectives to be satisfied by the outcome, all of the results to be sought. Likewise, the range and scope of the available alternatives can be artificially constrained. Bayes Theorem, Probability Theory, and Utility Theory tools are practical only in situations in which a limited number of readily quantifiable variables are involved. Considering their often limited scope of applicability, their complexity, and the time required to use most of these tools, few managers have ever taken the time to master them and continually apply them.

The Decision Analysis process developed in Chapter 5 and expanded in this chapter is a universally applicable, easily mastered tool that—most important—forces decision makers to think about objectives before thinking about alternatives. The goal of this process is for you, the decision maker, to define utopia yourself through objectives and then see how close you can come to meeting it, rather than letting mediocrity be defined by the capabilities of one or more (pet?) alternatives.

11

Potential Future Change—Opportunities and Disasters

In Chapter 7, we discussed the micro application of Potential Problem Analysis used in analyzing Implementation Plans. This chapter describes the macro application of Potential Problem Analysis and Potential Opportunity Analysis. In the macro mode, these tools are used to examine the ongoing conduct of the organization's affairs for undesirable or desirable Unplanned Future Change. The only differences between Potential Problem Analysis and Potential Opportunity Analysis are whether the searcher is casting a negative or a positive spin on Unplanned Future Change and trying to prevent or promote its occurrence.

The whole key to macro Potential Problem Analysis and Potential Opportunity Analysis, like micro Potential Problem Analysis, is detection. If an Unplanned Future Change is not detected, nothing can be done to attempt to prevent or promote it. On rare occasions, you might read or hear something that instantly rings a bell: "That could hurt—or help—us." Your subsequent thought is: "I need to do something about that." Fine and dandy, except that by then you're probably in the *reaction* mode. If the change was negative, it's probably too late to attempt to prevent it. If the change was positive, you've lucked out; it happened without your encouragement—except that the golden opportunity to capitalize on it may be a little tarnished.

The Basic Technique

To effectively practice macro Potential Problem Analysis and Potential Opportunity Analysis requires discipline, a time commitment, and dedication. An hour a week, perhaps even an hour a month, can be sufficient. But if it's not an hour of completely uninterrupted time, an hour in which nothing else is on your mind, you'll never become good at it. The absence of such dedication doesn't say that you'll never luck out and hit on an important potential Unplanned Future Change; it does suggest that your batting average won't be great.

Here's a list of questions you can use during that hour when you commit yourself to working on Potential Problem Analysis and Potential Opportunity Analysis.

> What significant changes *have occurred* in the past month / year in:
>
> Your responsibility area?
> • What have been/might be their effects?
>
> Adjacent/surrounding responsibility areas?
> • How have/could they affect your area?
>
> The outside world (government, marketplace, competition, etc.)?
> • How have/could they affect your area?

An anxious Potential Future Change thinker might ask, "Why think only about the past month or year? Why not the past week or month?" The answer is that except for abrupt natural disasters, significant changes seldom occur overnight; instead they grow over time. Few people are gifted at being able to see creeping change at its inception. Thus they need to examine a reasonably long period of time to notice change occurring.

After answering the questions about the past, turn your attention to the future and ask these questions:

> What significant changes *might occur* in the next few months / years in:
>
> Your responsibility area?
> • What could be their effects?
>
> Adjacent/surrounding responsibility areas?
> • How could they affect your area?
>
> The outside world (government, marketplace, competition, etc.)?
> • How could they affect your area?

If you're committed to the pursuit of identifying Unplanned Future Change, turn these questions into a form or worksheet that works for you. Then set aside a quiet, uninterrupted time each month for reflection and "fill in the blanks." Don't anticipate an immediate reward; don't expect to find a eureka in your first couple of attempts. It will take you that long just to get into the swing of considering the potential for change.

Forecasting, Predicting, Scenario Planning

Forecasting, predicting, scenario planning, and the like are underlying elements of Potential Problem Analysis and Potential Opportunity Analysis. The processes wouldn't succeed without them—that's what the Potential Problems and Likely Causes steps accomplish. However, don't forget that the underlying purposes of Potential Problem Analysis and Potential Opportunity Analysis are to improve control over the future. I'm a firm believer in the precepts that "To the extent that we can control the future we do not have to forecast it. . . . To the extent that we can respond rapidly and effectively to changes that we neither control nor expect . . . we need not forecast them. The better we can adapt to what we do not control, the less we need to control."[1]

I'm also a believer in forecasting, scenario planning, and similar tools so long as they are applied in moderation. With today's rapid pace of change, any attempt to look a decade ahead—for some industries even five years may be stretching practicality—exceeds the bounds of moderation. The value of such efforts lies in the mental exercise, the mind stretching and opening of people to new vistas, that takes place; it does *not* lie in the potential reality of any pictures or prognostications that are created as the result of such efforts. In other words, its value is in learning to expect the unexpected, in thinking in advance about how one might attempt to prevent, promote, or react to the unexpected.

Potential Problem Analysis in Action

The value and validity of this view were illustrated by Royal Dutch/Shell's ability to react to a more than 50% drop in the price of crude oil in the beginning of 1986. About two years prior to that catastrophic happening, the company's top management had played out a similar scenario.[2] In 1984, the price of crude oil was $28 a barrel. Those in the planning function at Royal Dutch/Shell felt it was not a zero probability that, within the next few years, the price of crude oil could plummet dramatically—perhaps by as much as 50%. They also felt that this would be tumultuous. However,

Shell's senior management wasn't interested in considering such an "absurd" turn of events.

Consequently, the Shell planners took another tack. They constructed a scenario that transported Shell's senior management two years ahead, specifically to April 1986. They were told that at that time the price of crude oil would be $15 a barrel, and they were asked to respond to three questions:

1. What do you think the government will do?
2. What do you think the competition will do?
3. What, if anything, will you do?

Apparently Shell's management saw this exercise as a game; it was one they were willing to play, to go along with, and perhaps even—consciously or subconsciously—learn from. The real-world event was that, by April 1986, the price of crude oil had plummeted to $10 a barrel. "The fact that Shell had already visited the world of $15 oil helped a great deal in that panicky spring of 1986."[3]

While the Shell planners were definitely pursuing the question "What significant changes *might occur* in the next few months or years in the outside world (government, marketplace, competition, etc.)?," they probably did not employ all the Potential Problem Analysis steps in their effort. Specifically, it's doubtful that they pursued the Preventive Actions step—and not doing this may have been reasonable. After all, could one company ever do anything to remove the likely causes or reduce the probability of such an enormous, global change? But never say never; you'll never know if you don't try.

In addition, it appears that Shell looked at the potential happening from a Potential Problem Analysis perspective. Management seemed to regard it as an undesirable happening. What if they had looked at it as a desirable happening or an opportunity? What if management analyzed it from a Potential Opportunity Analysis perspective? Suppose the company had been able to *promote* or speed up its happening; suppose its management had identified the event's likely causes and had been able to expedite their occurrence? Who knows what Shell could have reaped if it had been even further ahead of its competitors than it was?

Potential Opportunity Analysis in Action

Let's go back to the question "What significant changes *might occur* in the next few months or years in the outside world (government, marketplace, competition, etc.)?" again. If you were an executive in the airline industry back in 1982, you would have been well aware of the fact that Braniff

Airlines was hurting. Thus you might have said that a significant change that might occur in the next few months was that Braniff could go under. When you asked the question "How could they (it) affect your area?," you would have realized that Braniff's demise could offer an excellent opportunity for some carriers to expand their route structures.

Readers who were frequent flyers at that time may recall that Braniff "owned" the Dallas/Fort Worth airport; they dominated its gates and flight slots. And don't forget that, back in those days, the airlines were regulated by the FAA; the FAA controlled ticket prices, which airlines could fly where, and so on. At that time, United Airlines didn't have route authorization to fly out of Dallas/Fort Worth.

- At 4:00 P.M. Central time on 13 May 1982, Braniff announced that it was discontinuing operations.
- At 4:18 P.M. Central time that same day, United Airlines called the FAA and requested—and received—emergency route authorization to operate out of Dallas/Fort Worth.
- At 7:53 P.M. Central time that night, a United jet left Chicago's O'Hare airport for Dallas with complete station staffing: flight crews, mechanics, baggage handlers, counter and gate people, and so on.
- At 8:09 P.M. Pacific time, a United jet left Los Angeles for Dallas with a complete load of station equipment, including tow trucks, food service equipment, computer terminals, baggage carts, signs, paper clips, pens, ticket stock, and so on.
- At 10:10 P.M. Central time, the Chicago flight landed at Dallas—and had to borrow a gate from Frontier Airlines to unload its people.
- At 7:30 A.M. Central time on 14 May, the first United flight left Dallas—with one passenger on board.

Now you know very well that some executive at United didn't learn of Braniff's announcement at 4:01 P.M. on 13 May and only then get the bright idea to start rounding up people and equipment and head for Dallas. The potential opportunity, and the potential response to it, had been identified and thought out far in advance of the event—with the full realization that it might never happen.

I strongly doubt that United made any moves to attempt to promote this particular opportunity, Braniff's demise. However, it certainly made the right moves to prepare to instantly react to the event—*if* it happened. Moreover, it's not impossible that Braniff would still be flying today if its management had done some Potential Problem Analysis earlier in its own life cycle.

Crisis Planning

Over the past decade, much has been written about crisis or disaster planning. Some choose to differentiate between a crisis and a disaster, assigning the latter term to occurrences in nature. However, I'm going to treat these terms as synonymous. The bottom line is that, whatever you call such planning, it's nothing other than the macro application of Potential Problem Analysis. However, much of the popular literature on the subject focuses heavily on the "how to react to a crisis" mode—how to minimize the effects, the seriousness, of the crisis—and lightly on the "how to prevent a crisis" mode—how to minimize the probability of a crisis.

The real payoff in crisis planning comes from reducing the probability of the event. However, there's often one big catch to doing this—it can cost money. It's doubtful that someone in the pharmaceutical industry hadn't considered the possibility of "product tampering" long before the Tylenol crisis happened. However, to have done something earlier to reduce its probability would likely have been seen only as increasing costs. And then there's also the possibility that removing capsule versions—the product form tampered with in the Tylenol case—of products from the market would also have reduced sales.

The practical side of crisis planning is that probability cannot be reduced to zero. (Notice that the regulatory response to the Tylenol tampering was to require "tamper-*resistant*" packaging, not "tamper-*proof*"—which will never [?] be achieved.) However, to maximize the effectiveness of crisis planning, use *all* the Potential Problem Analysis tools, including the steps of Likely Causes and Preventive Actions. Don't be satisfied with just planning Contingent Actions.

The Visionary Mode

Another way to use the fundamental Unplanned Future Change concepts involves a composite of the Potential Problem Analysis and Potential Opportunity Analysis tools. A good name for it is the "visionary mode" because it's a technique that has appeal only to the visionary type of person, to the individual who has the interest, perseverance, and inclination to invest time in looking into the future to attempt to discover potential change that could impact his or her organization, whether positively or negatively.

To pursue this course, you must first compile a list of the significant elements that influence, or have the potential to influence, the future of your organization or business as it presently exists. This list should focus on external factors—on elements that are beyond the organization's walls and generally beyond its control. Above all, the items on the list should be defined at a macro level. To keep the effort from becoming unwieldy and cumbersome, the list should not contain more than ten items, with about five being preferable.

The purist might argue that limiting the list to significant elements is inappropriate, if not dangerous, because it requires making value judgments; this purist might argue for including all elements. If you work for a think tank and have plenty of time to contemplate the world's possibilities, you might find this an agreeable task. If you don't have infinite time available, then you recognize the pragmatic value of looking for the "significant."

Once your list of significant elements has been compiled, apply the Potential Problem Analysis and Potential Opportunity Analysis questions delineated earlier in this chapter to it, using them to dissect the significant elements in depth. My recommendation would be that you don't do this more often than quarterly. If you perform it too frequently, there's a chance you'll become too close to the situation and not be able to see the forest for the trees; you'll lose the distance, the stranger value, that is so necessary for the process to work. Above all, be sure to keep a written record of each session so that, perhaps every year or so, you can look back for trends in your thinking that might help improve your visionary perceptions.

Give the Visionary Mode a Try

Many of today's trends such as:

- The increasing use of outsourcing
- The increasing use of contract or part-time or temporary employees
- The increasing rate of technology change
- The increasing desire of workers to have more say in how they do their jobs
- The rise of virtual organizations
- The decrease in inventory levels
- The increase in the offering of customized products
- The globalization of markets
- The increase in leisure time
- The need for lifelong education
- And so on ad infinitum

offer golden opportunities to potentially benefit from this macro application of Potential Problem Analysis and Potential Opportunity Analysis.
Think about it! Why don't you give it a try?

12

On Creativity

The need for creativity in today's world is critical. We have seen how creativity is vital in the logical thought processes discussed throughout this book. When you are in the Decision Analysis develop mode creating ideas for new products, for example—or in the determine mode trying to come up with a new organization structure—certain fundamentals of creative thinking can make the difference between mediocre and outstanding solutions.

The intent of this chapter is to give a quick overview of those fundamentals that can be helpful. The chapter does *not* go into a detailed example of how the ideas are actually put to use because that depth would amount to a book unto itself.

Dozens of books have been written about creativity, espousing hundreds of ideas about it. Probably the most widely recognized creativity tool is brainstorming. Brainstorming is often labeled—by those who aren't aware of the concept of Past/Future/ Planned/Unplanned Change—a problem-solving tool. Brainstorming is no such thing—it is a tool for creating ideas and generating alternatives. Likewise, the day-one deviation concept discussed in Chapter 10 is a similar tool.

A Perspective on Creativity

Webster's defines the word "create" as "to bring into being; cause to exist; produce; specifically to evolve from one's own thought or imagination."[1] What does this have to do with the world of business? Well, it goes back to the old story of there being three kinds of people in this world: those who make things happen; those who watch things happen; and those who don't know anything is happening. Very simply, managers, engineers, scientists, and many others within an organization are paid to make new and better things happen, to bring into being new ideas. Whether their ideas are for new and better products, manufacturing processes, marketing approaches, organization structures, people relationships, or whatever, a significant component of their paychecks involves the expectation that they will make tomorrow better than yesterday. To the degree that they succeed, they succeed by being creative. And it's fairly safe to say that the more creative they are, the more they and their organizations will succeed.

Creativity takes on many hues: Picasso is recognized as a creative artist, Ernest Hemingway as a creative writer, Leonard Bernstein as a creative musician, Einstein as a creative scientist. So what about the world of business? Certainly Ray Kroc, the founder of McDonald's, was a creative manager. Kelly Johnson, of Lockheed's Skunk Works renown, is widely recognized as a creative engineer. Steve Jobs and Steve Wozniak of Apple Computer fame certainly earned the label of being creative business people. Creativity exists in business just as it does in the arts; it's just not as widely recognized and publicized.

The Literature on Creativity

Creativity is often perceived as a mystical, elusive ether. One of the reasons it seems so elusive is that the literature on the subject is often lacking. There is much discussion about it, but little on *how to do it*. The literature is loaded with all kinds of games and puzzles that, if you successfully complete them, are supposed to suggest that you're creative.

So what's the purpose? The puzzles seem intended to shame you into admitting that failure to complete them is a failure of creativity and that this lack of creativity is all your fault because you don't think right. But, unfortunately, there are seldom many specifics offered about how one might alter his or her mental processes to think more creatively. The literature seems to thrive on making creativity seem complex. It does a poor job of teaching people the simplicity of creativity, of encouraging them to see things differently and think about them differently. Much of it treats creativity as an end unto itself when it really is a means to an end. Creativity in business is a means to better products, manufacturing processes, organization structures, promotional programs, and on and on. Creativity can be impossible or it can be simple, according to your mind-set. Creativity can be impossible if you will it to be so. Creativity can be simple if you will just allow it to be so.

Creativity in the Business World

For eons, philosophers have pontificated about creativity as an intangible abstraction. In their world, and for their horizons, this may be a wonderful exercise. For the world of business, it does nothing. For the world of business to benefit from whatever creativity is and whatever it has to offer, it must think about creativity in terms of practical, everyday application.

Often in the business world, creativity is first thought of as something associated with new products. Without a doubt, this is an area in which creativity can reign supreme. However, creativity is as important in every other facet of an organization as it is in the new product area. To develop a perspective on creativity that relates only to the new product area would be tremendous disservice to you, the reader. Why? Because the fundamentals of creativity in business cover the entire spectrum of business functions.

For the executive, the engineer, the machine operator, and the organization, creativity is worthless unless it leads to new and better ways or products that the marketplace will buy or that will make us more productive or that could be a stepping stone toward improving profitability.

Today, creativity is discussed as though it's synonymous with entrepreneurship and high technology. Certainly, it's safe to say that most entrepreneurs are creative. Many of them earned that description because they were the first with an idea, a new product, a new service, a new mode of distribution, or a new whatever. However, according to Peter Drucker in his landmark book *Innovation and Entrepreneurship*,[2] the majority of entrepreneurial discoveries are actually in low-tech fields. Drucker further shows that many billion-dollar corporations are just as entrepreneurial, just as creative, as the small start-ups.

Another common business perspective that needs to be put into its place as far as creativity is concerned is that of "need filling." This is a cherished term among marketers and new-product people. Find a need and then go out and fill it. Many companies do this very successfully. But that's not the epitome of new product creativity. "Want creating" is the height of new product creativity: creating an idea for something that people don't need; creating an idea that is so good that people can be made to want it. That's what Dr. Edwin Land did when he invented instant photography via the Polaroid® camera.

In today's world, if your paycheck isn't coming from creativity, it might not be coming for long. The presence or absence of creativity in a person or an organization is usually obvious. Take the 3M Company; *In Search of Excellence*[3] reported that it introduces over 100 major new products each year. Every year 3M adds at least one new division. And each year at least 25% of its sales come from products that didn't exist five years ago.

The Mind of the Strategist[4] reported that, for a decade, Toyota held its work force at about 45,000 people. Yet over this same period it increased its production of automobiles $2^1/_2$ times. How did the company accomplish this? It came from creativity—from an average of twenty improvement suggestions per employee per year. These suggestions produced savings of $230 million a year.

These are examples of creativity in action, piece by piece, one bit at a time. They are also examples of the cumulative effect of masses of creative happenings that fit together and build on each other. A mass of rocks strewn about the desert floor doesn't become a pyramid until the rocks are assembled.

Making Creativity Happen

Now that the case has been made for the value of creativity in the world of business, what's next? Every product that's made and every process that's used to manufacture the product has a sequence to it. True, these sequences are sometimes flexible. Depending on fluctuations in the available input or the desired output, many variations may exist in the sequence. But the fundamental point remains: effective results require an effective sequence. The same is true in creating ideas; an effective sequence for attempting to create ideas can go a long way toward raising the odds that effective results will be achieved. The balance of this chapter discusses a sequence of approach and thinking perspectives that can be helpful in creating ideas.

First, we'll take a look at *triggers for creativity*. Too often, people in business view creativity as something they should be able to turn on when desired. In other words, it's only useful when it's wanted. The business person who really wants to be creative should train himself or herself to become increasingly cognizant of the myriad of opportunities to be creative that pass by unannounced each day. Creativity in response to an opportunity dropped in one's lap is just as valuable as creativity that can be turned on at will.

When a person feels the need to turn on his or her creativity to assist in developing a solution to a problem, the most critical element of the whole process is knowing exactly what this will accomplish. So, we'll next explore *the definition of the problem.*

Once the creativity spotlight has been pointed to and focused on the target problem, the third element in the sequence is to remove or determine how to avoid the *barriers to creativity* that lie along the path.

Now the would-be creative person is ready for step four: *approaches to creativity.* He or she should now have prepared the way to tackle the practical elements of working on a creative idea.

Triggers for Creativity

How does Toyota obtain 900,000 suggestions for improvements from its employees each year? What are the triggers, the seemingly innocuous happenings that lead people to come up with their "ahas"? The triggers are everywhere. They are present, day in and day out, in everyday events. They are present in everyday dissatisfactions and in everyday thoughts about better satisfaction, thoughts about "Wouldn't it be great if. . . ."

Let's take a look at some of the triggers that history has recorded. While on vacation, Edwin Land took some pictures of his daughter. She asked why she couldn't see the results right then and there and wasn't happy with his response. That got him thinking about overcoming his daughter's dissatisfaction. Within an hour he had developed the concept of instant photography in his mind. You know the rest of the story.

Art Fry sang in a church choir. As many choir members did, he put slips of paper in his hymnal to mark each selection so he could find it quickly. The only problem was that the slips often fell out. Thus, his solution to the problem didn't always work. Taking his dissatisfaction back to his job and applying some scrounging time and resources to it, he developed what became 3M's Post-it™ note pads.

The widely acclaimed Japanese kanban system of just-in-time parts supply was developed because of dissatisfaction over the capital that was being tied up unproductively in parts inventories sitting on the shelf.

Teflon™ wasn't invented; it was the result of an accident. However, its subsequent application to a myriad of products happened because a curious chemist didn't throw away the accident—he played with it to learn more about its properties. He found better satisfactions that it could provide.

Whether it be creative application and better satisfactions, as in the case of Teflon™, or creative discovery and overcoming dissatisfactions, as in the case of the Polaroid Land® camera and Post-it™ note pads, the triggers were seemingly mundane occurrences. These exact same events probably happened to hundreds of other fathers and choir members and chemists. The only difference is they were triggers to these three people but events to be forgotten by the other hundreds.

The Trigger Factor

Basically, a trigger is set off by the mental resistance to taking something for granted or accepting it at face value. It's the mental discipline and curiosity needed to examine every event to see if it contains a "dissatisfaction factor"—to ask "Why?" and "How might this (dissatisfaction) be overcome?"

The inventor of intermittent windshield wipers for automobiles won a multimillion-dollar settlement from Detroit's automakers for their unauthorized expropriation of his invention. Collectively, the major automakers must have thousands of engineers on their payrolls and it's probably safe to say that most of them drive cars and that they have driven in the rain. Thus they must have experienced the exasperation of continually having to turn their windshield wipers on and off during a light rainfall. Not one of these "experts" saw this need as a dissatisfier; to them it was not a trigger. Herman Kahn once observed that experts often miss things because they are experts and, as a result, have ironclad perspectives that they cannot see beyond. He referred to this phenomenon as "educated incapacity." When people take themselves too seriously, they often become oblivious to the world as it passes by them. What might be seen as a significant event, as a trigger, by one person is mere background noise to the multitudes.

Every person in your organization is exposed to many such events every day and yet the vast majority are oblivious to these happenings. Some of these unrecognized—and thus unchallenged—dissatisfiers just might have fantastic new product potential.

What do you need to do to catch them as they go passing by? What must you do to turn them into triggers? It's simple—you just need to momentarily freeze each happening as it passes in review and ask yourself if there's any dissatisfaction buried in it. If there is, ask "Why?" "How might this be overcome?"

But if this is so simple, why didn't Art Fry invent Post-it™ notes the first time the paper markers fell from his hymnal? The answer is obvious. The first time it happened his dissatisfaction level was probably subconscious and he didn't recognize it—it didn't come up to the trigger factor level for him. Why? Well, I guess most people will put up with anything once, or twice, or . . . ?

You are exposed to many of these same kinds of triggers, perhaps dozens (hundreds?) of them every day. If you fail to notice them, or if you accept them as fleeting events, they will not be triggers. If you pause, think, reflect, and question them, you never can tell—one of them just might become a trigger.

The Definition of the Problem

It has often been said that "a problem correctly stated is half solved." To Edwin Land, the delay in seeing the results of his picture-taking session became a problem. The marketplace has seen the results of his statement of it.

To most people, the invention of the transistor at Bell Labs is probably thought to be the result of much luck at the end of some fanciful, far-out flight in a research laboratory. In fact, it was the consequence of a very specific problem. In constantly trying to reduce the physical size and power requirements of telephone switching equipment, engineers came to the point where they felt that the traditional electromechanical relay could be reduced no further. That led to a problem statement. The solution was the transistor.

Problems can often be solved by creating new ideas. If we accept the adage that a problem correctly stated is half solved, then the question obviously becomes, "How do I state the problem?"

In his book *The Art of Problem Solving*,[5] Russell Ackoff talks about a problem in developing the frozen-fish business in Britain. It seems that frozen fish had a flat taste and, after trying it once, British housewives wouldn't repeat the purchase. The fish company's scientists suggested either freezing the fish as soon as they were caught or keeping them alive until they reached the dock. Based on the economics of the two recommendations, the company converted the holds of its fishing fleet into pools where the fish were kept alive. However, the flat taste persisted. It was determined that their inactivity in the densely packed pool led to a chemical change in the fish.

The company saw the problem as, "How can we keep the fish active?" Many ideas were tried without success. One day a visitor, on learning of the problem quite by accident, suggested putting a predator in the pool. The flat taste problem was overcome at the trivial cost of a few fish consumed by the predator.

This brings us to a concept called the true choice, which was also mentioned in Chapter 5. It involves simply stating the problem at its most elementary level. It asks "What is the true choice we're faced with?" For example, one might make the case that the true choice in the flat-tasting fish problem was not "How can we keep the fish active?" Instead it was "How can we recreate/simulate the fish's natural environment?" since apparently an unnatural environment led to the flat taste. Such a problem statement might have more quickly led to examining the ways in which the pool was different from nature's environment.

In one of his books on lateral thinking, Edward de Bono talks about a problem in a large office building in which people were complaining about the length of time they had to wait for the elevators. In looking at the problem as "How can we speed up the elevators?" the building's owners felt they were up against a brick wall of prohibitive costs. They couldn't find an acceptable way out of the problem. In a triumph of lateral thinking, it was suggested that mirrors be placed on the walls around the elevators. People would thus spend the time admiring or grooming themselves and be oblivious to the wait. It worked.

However, suppose the problem had originally been stated in terms of the true choice: "How can we eliminate complaints about the elevators?" Speeding them up would have been an idea; mirrors might have been recognized as an idea, as well as mounting television sets on the wall, piping in news broadcasts, and so on.

There's another important point hidden in this elevator example: The problem was first looked at in terms of the need to create change in the *performance of the product* (the elevators) itself. The problem was solved by creating change in *how the product was perceived*, by creating change in the product's environment.

Barriers to Creativity

One of the most important steps in developing your creative abilities is to first recognize and own up to those things that stand in the way of coming up with creative ideas. The first and foremost of these barriers is *your experience*. David Ogilvy made the case very bluntly when he said: The majority of businessmen are incapable of original thought because they are unable to escape from the tyranny of reason.[6]

Your experience becomes your base for reasoning. In many circumstances your experience can be a valuable asset. In situations in which you are searching for creative ideas, it can be an excessive liability. Perhaps that's the reason why many breakthrough ideas are developed by people distant from the field in which the idea is created. They aren't encumbered by experience in that field. After all, Kenneth Olson, the founder and then president of Digital Equipment Corporation, relied on his extensive experience in computers when he told attendees at the World Future Society's 1977 convention: "There is no reason for any individual to have a computer in their home."[7] That was about the same time Steve Jobs and Steve Wozniak founded Apple Computer in their garage.

The *assumptions you make* can be another barrier to creativity. For years, some greeting-card companies labored under the assumption that their competition was other greeting-card companies. No doubt this affected and directed—and constrained—their creative efforts. However, the assumption was subsequently found to be way off base; the telephone company, FTD (Florists Telegraph Delivery), and the like were the really significant competition.

The *judgments you make* are a third barrier to coming up with creative ideas. When was the last time you very quickly reacted to an idea with: "It will never work," or "We tried that before," or "They'll never buy it"? Think about it. Recall judgments that were laughed at, like, "He'll fall off the end of the earth" (said about Christopher Columbus), or "They'll never replace horses" (said about automobiles), or "Birds were made to fly, not man" (said about airplanes).

And what about the judgments that are accepted as sound and valid today? What about Einstein's Theory of Relativity, $E = MC^2$? Could it be proven incorrect at some time in the future? Could today's acceptance of it be inhibiting somebody's creativity?

Think about the judgments of your business environment that are locked into your everyday thinking. Take out a sheet of paper and list some of them. Would you bet your job that they'll still be valid in five years, in five months?

Look at the American automotive industry, for example. To this day, Detroit still clings tightly to its judgment that a major model change every several years is mandatory for survival. How many decades ago was it that the Volkswagen Beetle on the low end and the Mercedes on the high end contradicted this myth?

Your *thinking patterns* can be another barrier to creativity. However, although thinking patterns can seriously inhibit creativity, you couldn't survive without them. Like your experience, they can be both an asset and a liability. The key lies in knowing when to depend on them and when to lock them in a closet. If you're driving down a highway and you hear a siren, a stored thinking pattern immediately takes over. It tells you to locate the source and, if it's in your line of travel, pull over to get out of the way of an emergency vehicle—or to receive your speeding ticket.

In his fascinating tape, *Software for the Brain*,[8] Count Michael de Saint-

Arnaud makes the point that if you were hungry and wanted to order a pizza, if you couldn't utilize your stored thinking patterns about pizza, it would take you a week to order it.

The speed with which thinking patterns can be established can also be either a tremendous asset or liability. Before you have installed the newly purchased smoke detector in your home, you've already installed a thinking pattern about it in your brain. You already know that the instant you hear it you should get out of the house, with the possible exceptions of calling the fire department and attempting to extinguish the fire yourself if circumstances permit.

A fifth barrier to creativity is what's known as the *right-answer syndrome.* Unfortunately, this syndrome is locked into most people's brains shortly after they start school. It's locked in because of the left-brained, get-the-right-answer construct of our educational system. Most school systems are superior at turning out automatons who can memorize and parrot back the right answer; they are inferior at turning out people who can think and create.

Answers are only arrangements of information. You're probably familiar with the game of tic-tac-toe. In it are nine boxes (Figure 12.1).

If you look at each box as containing a different piece of information, how many possible combinations are there of these nine pieces of information? Nine? Eighty-one? No, there are 362,880 possible combinations of these nine pieces of information. (The answer is 9', or 9 factorial, which means it is determined by multiplying 9 x 8 x 7 x 6 x 5 x 4 x 3 x 2 x 1 = 362,880.)

Answers come from arrangements of information. There are 362,880 possible arrangements of the nine numbers in the tic-tac-toe illustration. If, instead of numbers, each of the nine boxes contained a piece of information, an idea relating to a potential new product, there would be 362,880 ways in which these ideas could be arranged.

Given all the possible combinations of information that can be present in a situation, it may be a bit presumptuous to say that your creative prob-

1	2	3
4	5	6
7	8	9

Figure 12.1   Tic-Tac-Toe Illustration

lem solving has produced the *right* answer. It might be safer to say it's a good answer, or that it's better than any of the other answers that have been thought up, but to say unequivocally that it's the best might be more an exhibition of ignorance than competence.

The last major barrier to creativity we'll discuss is *fear of failure*. Failure is actually a great contributor to creativity; it's a tremendous learning tool. Unfortunately, too many managers are graduates of the right-answer school and are oblivious to the value of failure. Entrepreneurs were discussed earlier. Entrepreneurs and entrepreneurial organizations are said to achieve success because they take risks. However, if those risks don't also produce some failures then, by definition, there's more playing-it-safe present than risk taking.

Of course, excessive failures that aren't learned from can spell disaster. It's not a black or white, but a shades of gray situation. Don't fear failure — use it as a learning tool.

Perhaps the epitome of this perspective was expressed by Thomas Edison. When a friend suggested that Edison's attempts to develop an electric storage battery were obviously a failure since he had tried thousands of materials without success, Edison replied: "Why, man, I've got a lot of results. I know several thousand things that won't work."[9]

The value of failure was recognized by IBM's Thomas J. Watson when he said: "The way to succeed is to double your failure rate."[10] It seemed to work for him.

A closing thought on barriers to creativity comes from Count Michael de Saint-Arnaud: The more intelligent people are, the less likely they are to be good thinkers.[11] Why? Because your intelligence can be the kingpin of your barriers to creativity. When it comes to being creative, you can be your own worst enemy.

Approaches to Creativity

It's necessary to face up to the reality of creativity barriers before looking at approaches to creativity. As stated earlier, creativity can be simple, if you will just allow it to be so. It can only be simple if you first confront its inhibitors and gain control over them.

I've found that the path to creative ideas has three brightly illuminated signs. Their messages are:

1. Forget everything you know (the relationships).
2. Remember everything you know (the pieces).
3. Rearrange everything you know (same pieces, new relationships).

The key to understanding the message on the first sign comes from Pablo Picasso: "Every act of creation is first of all an act of destruction."[12] As we emphasized earlier, answers come from arrangements of information. However, virtually all the information you carry around in your memory bank, and which you tap when faced with a problem, is tied together in relationships. Roger von Oech astutely observed that "as people grow older, they become prisoners of familiarity"[13] (of relationships). The first step in attempting to create ideas is to destroy the familiarity—the relationships—of everything you know about a problem.

Back in the 1940s before Edwin Land invented instant photography, every consumer was well aware that seeing the results of a picture-taking session was related to developing the film, which was related to a place called a darkroom, which was related to their local drugstore as its contact point. Everybody was a prisoner of that familiarity, including Edwin Land, until he broke its shackles and let his mind sever those relationships.

Once this act of destruction takes place, you are left with a rich reservoir of bits and pieces of information, a vast storehouse of unconnected facts and fantasies, thoughts and ideas. However, just like the words in a dictionary, they do nothing until they are selected and assembled to become a coherent sum.

The value possessed by these pieces is summed up by the late Nobel Prize-winning biochemist Albert Szent-Gyorgyi: Discovery consists of seeing what everybody has seen—and thinking what nobody thought.[14] More than likely, most of the pieces of the problem you're looking at are the same pieces that others are looking at. The pieces are the means to the end, but they are valueless as they stand. Thus the key to a better idea, "thinking something different," takes us to the last step.

The final step is to search for new ways of assembling the pieces, to seek new relationships among them. The value and simplicity of this step were succinctly described by the English painter Sir Joshua Reynolds: "Invention is little more than new combinations of those images which have been previously gathered and deposited in the memory."[15]

Edwin Land forged a new combination of his images of a camera and a darkroom. Art Fry saw a new connection between the adhesives technology possessed by his employer and his falling slips of paper.

There are a myriad of techniques developed over the years that are supposed to foster the creative process and help create ideas. These range from the well-known brainstorming developed by Alex Osborne in 1938, through morphology developed by Cal Tech's Fritz Zwichy, to Edward de Bono's lateral thinking, and to catalog techniques, checklists, the use of metaphors, and so on *ad infinitum*.

The fact that Arthur VanGundy's *Techniques of Structured Problem Solving*[16] lists all of the above plus fifty more is ample testimony to the fact that the Rosetta stone of creativity is yet to be found. Yet virtually all these techniques are simply variations on the theme of destroying the relationships and assembling the pieces in new ways.

When attempting to solve a problem, create ideas, or respond to some other motivation or stimulus, the last thing you should do is try to create an idea—*the* idea. Instead, develop as many ideas as you can, and then pick and choose. As Emile Chartier expressed it, "Nothing is more dangerous than an idea when it is the only one you have."[17]

Although creativity can be simple, this is not necessarily synonymous with being easy or painless. Walter Bagehot noted that "one of the greatest pains to human nature is the pain of a new idea."[18] Nobody said it would always be easy. After all, if it was, would your job exist?

Revisiting Part II

In the chapter on Decision Analysis, we noted that there's little room for creativity in the select mode. In this type of Decision Analysis, the alternatives are usually well-known, off-the-shelf options. However the determine and develop modes offer exceptional opportunities for creating new ideas, new alternatives, and new ways of fulfilling objectives that have never been thought of before (Figure 12.2).

In Potential Problem Analysis, particularly in the Identify Likely Causes and Develop Preventive Actions steps, the ideas that have been discussed in this chapter can be extremely helpful (Figure 12.3).

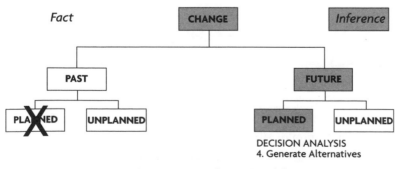

Figure 12.2   Change Model 4A

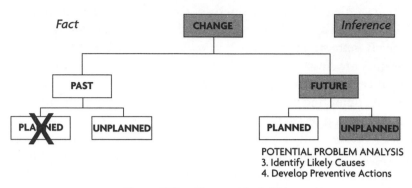

POTENTIAL PROBLEM ANALYSIS
3. Identify Likely Causes
4. Develop Preventive Actions

Figure 12.3   Change Model 5A

Summary

Here is a simple summation of the fundamental steps in developing your creative thinking capabilities:

- Barriers—stop being your own worst enemy.
- Forget everything you know (the relationships).
- Remember everything you know (the pieces).
- Rearrange everything you know (same pieces, new relationships).

The marketer, the engineer, the lathe operator, and everyone else approach the tasks of their jobs via particular sequences that they have learned and fine-tuned over the years. Likewise, these and all other types of people in the world of business can do the same for the creative elements of their jobs.

Practice, practice, and a little more practice is the name of the game. But remember, all the practice in the world will never give you a batting average of 1.000. And, as you are well aware, not even the most successful players in the game need a batting average remotely close to that perfect number to be winners. But they never stop trying to improve their record.

An Annotated Bibliography

Of the over fifty books on creativity in my library, the following are the winners:

Arthur B. VanGundy, *Techniques of Structured Problem Solving* (New York: Van Nostrand Reinhold, 1981). A collection of over fifty detailed, how-to descriptions of a variety of thinking processes.

Roger von Oech, *A Whack on the Side of the Head* (New York, Warner Books, 1983). An offbeat, humorous, attention-getting collection of do's and don'ts that serve to effectively open the reader's mind.

Michael Michalko, *Cracking Creativity* (Berkeley, CA: Ten Speed Press, 1998). A reduction into everyday language of how many of history's most creative people generated their ideas.

Michael Michalko, *Thinkertoys* (Berkeley, CA: Ten Speed Press, 1991). This is my all-time favorite. Over thirty short and eminently readable chapters introduce a broad variety of thinking tools.

James Webb Young, *A Technique for Producing Ideas* (Chicago: Crain Books, 1984). The shortest book on creativity you'll ever see. A simple, pragmatic, fundamental discussion of how to think more creatively. Originally published in 1940, it is described as "*The* classic on creative thinking."

Appendix

Problem-Solving Worksheets

Decision Analysis
DECISION ANALYSIS WORKSHEET

Implementation Planning
PLAN COMPONENTS WORKSHEET
PLAN EVENTS AND TIMES WORKSHEET
TIME ALLOCATION WORKSHEET
PLAN OBJECTIVES TEST WORKSHEET

Potential Problem Analysis
POTENTIAL PROBLEMS WORKSHEET
LIKELY CAUSES WORKSHEET
ACTIONS WORKSHEET

Problem Analysis
PROBLEM ANALYSIS WORKSHEET

Decision Analysis Worksheet

DECISION STATEMENT:

OBJECTIVES	WT	ALTERNATIVES																										
		A			B			C			D			E			F			G			H			I		
		SC	WT	SC	SC	WT	SC	SC	WT	SC	SC	WT	SC	SC	WT	SC	SC	WT	SC	SC	WT	SC	SC	WT	SC	SC	WT	SC
TOTAL WEIGHTED SCORE																												

Plan Components Worksheet

PLAN STATEMENT:		
COMPONENTS	DEPENDS ON	WHO?

Plan Events and Times Worksheet

PLAN STATEMENT:					
TIME PERIOD	**EVENTS—PLANNED**		**EVENTS—ACTUAL**		**Why the deviation?**
	Start	Finish	Start	Finish	

Time Allocation Worksheet

MONTH												
WEEK PERSON	1	2	3	4	1	2	3	4	1	2	3	4

Each week assumes 4 days available:

= 4 days   = 3 days   = 2 days   = 1 day

Plan Objectives Test Worksheet

PLAN STATEMENT:				
RESOURCE		Total amount available:		
COMPONENTS		Amount Required	Cumulative	Actual

Potential Problems Worksheet

PLAN/SITUATION STATEMENT:			
POTENTIAL PROBLEMS	P	S	AR
A			
B			
C			
D			
E			
F			
G			
H			
I			
J			
K			
L			
M			
N			

Likely Causes Worksheet

PLAN/SITUATION STATEMENT:		
POTENTIAL PROBLEM:	P	S
LIKELY CAUSES	P	AR
1		
2		
3		
4		
5		
6		
7		
8		
9		
10		
11		
12		
13		
14		

Actions Worksheet

PLAN/SITUATION STATEMENT:					
POTENTIAL PROBLEM:				P	S
LIKELY CAUSES		P	PREVENTIVE ACTIONS	WHO	RP
CONTINGENT ACTION:			TRIGGER:		WHO

Problem Analysis Worksheet

DEVIATION STATEMENT:

	IS	IS NOT	DIFFERENCES	CHANGES (TIMING)	TEST
WHAT Defect Object					
WHERE Observed On					
WHEN Observed On					
EXTENT How bad How many					

POSSIBLE
CAUSE
HYPOTHESES

HOW VERIFY MOST PROBABLE CAUSE:

Notes

CHAPTER 1

1. Ben Heirs, *The Professional Decision Thinker* (New York: Dodd Mead, 1986).
2. Gary Hamel and C. K. Prahalad, *Competing for the Future* (Boston: Harvard Business School Press, 1994).
3. Edward de Bono, "Thinking in America . . . the Lost Art," *Critical Intelligence*, October 1994.
4. Melvin Zimet and Ronald G. Greenwood, *The Evolving Science of Management* (New York: AMACOM, 1979).
5. Benjamin B. Tregoe and John W. Zimmerman, *Top Management Strategy* (New York: Simon & Schuster, 1980).
6. Ibid.
7. Ibid.
8. Ibid.
9. Ibid.
10. *The International Webster's New Encyclopedic Dictionary of the English Language* (Chicago: The English Language Institute of America, 1975).

CHAPTER 3

1. *The International Webster's New Encyclopedic Dictionary of the English Language* (Chicago: The English Language Institute of America, 1975).
2. Ibid.

CHAPTER 4

1. Stephen R. Covey, *First Things First* (New York: Simon & Schuster, 1984).

CHAPTER 8

1. Charles H. Kepner and Benjamin B. Tregoe, *The Rational Manager* (New York: McGraw-Hill, 1965).
2. Herbert A. Simon, *The New Science of Management Decision* (Englewood Cliffs, NJ: Prentice-Hall, 1977).

CHAPTER 9

1. Walter Kiechel III, "How to Lead a Meeting," *Fortune*, 29 August 1988.
2. Henry Holtzman, "Why Do We Keep MEETING Like This?," *Modern Office Procedures*, August 1983.
3. John E. Tropman and Kathryn A. Kozaitis, *Playing by the Rules: Meeting the Challenge of High Quality Decisions* (Austin, TX: 3M Meeting Management Institute, 1991).
4. Maria Fisher, "Why Are We Meeting Like This?," *Forbes*, 16 January 1984.

CHAPTER 11

1. Russell L. Ackoff, *Creating the Corporate Future* (New York, John Wiley, 1981).
2. Arie P. de Geus, "Planning as Learning," *Harvard Business Review*, March-April 1988.
3. Ibid.

CHAPTER 12

1. *The International Webster's New Encyclopedic Dictionary of the English Language* (Chicago: The English Language Institute of America, 1975).
2. Peter F. Drucker, *Innovation and Entrepreneurship* (New York: Harper & Row, 1985).
3. Thomas J. Peters and Robert H. Waterman, Jr., *In Search of Excellence* (New York: Harper & Row, 1982).
4. Kenichi Ohmae, *The Mind of the Strategist* (New York: McGraw-Hill, 1982).
5. Russell L. Ackoff, *The Art of Problem Solving* (New York: John Wiley, 1978).
6. Thomas J. Peters and Robert A. Waterman, Jr., op. cit.
7. Christopher Cerf and Victor Navasky, *The Experts Speak* (New York: Pantheon Books, 1984).
8. Michael de Saint-Arnaud, *Software for the Brain* (New York: CVS to BVS The Company Inc., 1985).
9. Frank Lewis Dyer and Thomas Commerford Martin, *Edison: His Life and Inventions* (New York: Harper Brothers, 1910).
10. Roger von Oech, *A Whack on the Side of the Head* (New York: Warner Books, 1983).
11. Michael de Saint-Arnaud, op. cit.
12. Roger von Oech, op. cit.
13. Ibid.
14. Irving Good, *The Scientist Speculates* (London: Heinemann, 1962).
15. Ted Goodman, *The Forbes Book of Business Quotations* (New York: Black Dog & Leventhal Publishers, 1997).
16. Arthur B. VanGundy, Jr., *Techniques of Structured Problem Solving* (New York: Van Nostrand Reinhold, 1981).
17. Roger von Oech, op. cit.
18. *The Oxford Dictionary of Quotations* (New York: Oxford University Press, 1992).

Index